D1555749

# PHASE 7 SWING

# PHASE

# 7 SWING

## Reeves Weedon
Fellow of the P.G.A.

*To Anthony,*
*A Star pupil !*
*Keep believing*
*Reeves*

**A MOUNTAIN LION BOOK**

Library of Congress Control Number 2012932043

ISBN 978-0-9839689-0-0

*Phase 7 Swing* is a registered trademark.

Manufactured in the United States of America
10  9  8  7  6  5  4  3  2  1

Book design by Bob Antler, Antler Designworks

MOUNTAIN LION BOOKS
9 Voorhees Court
Pennington, New Jersey 08534

To Sue:

*Can't make it on my own—I build my dreams around you.*

# Foreword

You might ask, "Where would a prodigious driver of the ball go to increase the length of his drives that customarily exceed 400 yards?"

When I posed this question to Lee Cox, my regular golf swing coach, he responded, "I think Reeves Weedon can help you."

So I asked Reeves to help me not only with my length but also with my accuracy. The fact of the matter is that a world champion driver of the ball—I am the 2010 RE/MAX World Long Drive Champion (won with a drive of 414 yards)—needs to keep improving, just like all golfers. Competition is fierce. The performance gap among the top competitors is miniscule. My coach had studied with Reeves and knew that his techniques were solidly grounded in science; thus, he felt Reeves would at the very least do no harm. My coach was also aware that Reeves had successfully helped literally hundreds of golfers of all abilities—from beginners to scratch players—with the principles he taught in *Phase 7 Swing*.

Reeves suggested that my body mass would move quicker if I maintained a better connection with the ground. Thus, he taught me a pronounced front-to-back/back-to-front weight shift—a technique he called the transverse body pivot. This kept me centered and minimized any power leakage. It gave me a feeling of pushing down on the backswing and pushing up and off the ground on the downswing. [Note: this pushing was a feeling, the result of a powerful turning of my core as my weight shifted back and forth. In actual execution my feet do not leave the ground till the ball is in flight.] This connection is rooted in Newton's third law, but I'll let Reeves explain this to you in the book (Chapter 4).

Reeves also encouraged me to keep my left arm under my right shoulder, a position that would allow me to rotate quicker. This promotes two other feelings that I like. The first is that I'm literally hitting the ball with my body and the arms are just going along for the ride. And secondly, I feel that I can turn as hard and as swiftly as possible and the clubhead will strike the ball dead, solid perfect—which to me means long and straight.

The bottom line is that I'm hitting the ball farther than ever. In the 2011 world long drive competition I drove the ball 452 yards, an increase just shy of ten percent (10%).

My coach and I keep in periodic contact with Reeves so I can keep tapping into his teaching ideas. I want to keep improving. If you want to improve your overall game and to increase your distance and accuracy—off the tee and everywhere on the course—use *Phase 7 Swing*. I am a world champion and I know it works.

Joe Miller
2010 RE/MAX World
Long Drive Champion

# Acknowledgments

Professionally, I am indebted to David Lee of Gravity Golf. It all changed when I met you—you are an inspiration. Ian Clark, thank you for your enthusiasm, and multiple thanks to Kingsley Webb, Mac O'Grady, and to the many proponents of The Golfing Machine for your knowledge. Many thanks to Nathan, Chris, Neil and Seve—I can't do it without you.

I am much obliged for the help of Joe Miller, 2010 RE/MAX Long Drive Champion, who wrote the foreword and demonstrated that his powerful drives could improve with the principles of Phase 7 Swing. Thanks to Lloyd Pestell of Courage Media, James Pulaski for the great photographs and to David Ginn and Gavin Skinner for demonstrating Phase 7 Swing, and to two superb golf clubs that provided the facilities for taking the photographs, Hartsbourne Country Club and Hopewell Valley Golf Club. I would also like to acknowledge the board and members of Hartsbourne Country Club, where it a privilege to work and teach.

I very much appreciate the wise business advice of Daren Olley and John Monk, the editing skills of Peter Kollmann, the expert book design skills of Bob Antler, Antler Designworks, and John Monteleone, friend and publisher of Mountain Lion Books—without you, there would be no book.

Most of all I am deeply grateful to my family. Mum, Dad and Gramp—thank you for your unconditional love and ongoing support. Sue, Daniel, Amelia and Sophia—I love you so much. You are truly a blessing.

# Contents

# Introduction

I have spent a lot of time studying the teachings of many of the world's top golf instructors. The result of this educational journey was what you might expect: there were as many ideas on how to swing a golf club as there were instructors. I concluded that although each instructor offered a viable way of learning the golf swing, only a smattering of the golf world's elite swing thinkers overtly based their systems on the bedrock of scientific laws. The laws were operating in the background as sure as the law of gravity was responsible for dropping that infamous apple on Sir Isaac Newton's noggin but they were rarely acknowledged. And when it came to any crossroads where science converged with opinion, science—as it applied to or explained the golf swing—was always the road less traveled.

This reluctance of my fellow teaching pros to turning over his or her knowledge of the golf swing to a third party, that is, the scientists and their kit bags of irrefutable laws, seemed predictable. This pedagogical phenomenon is simply a matter of human nature, as most of us love our own inventions and insights more dearly than what others have discovered. Also at work is that many good teachers who understand very well the science of the swing don't teach it simply because they don't think their students need to know this information.

Phase 7 Swing is different because it is based in great part on science, the laws of force and motion, and my desire that my students understand how the laws of motion are being harnessed in Phase 7 Swing instruction. I firmly believe that when Phase 7 Swing techniques harness the explosive payload of these laws they deliver the most consistent and powerful ballstriking. So fasten your seat belt, you're about to take off on a rocket ride to great golf.

The book you're holding in your hands is not only a journey that explores new frontiers in golf instruction but also a trip that takes us "back to the future." I make this statement because I have selectively culled and unabashedly embraced the swing instructions of legendary players such as Ben Hogan and Jack Nicklaus and pioneering instructors such as Percy Boomer, Homer Kelley and Harvey Penick, focusing on their swing techniques that in some way or another comply with the laws of motion or other laws that govern the physical world in which we live. These insights provide many of the foundation blocks upon which I've constructed the teachings tenets of Phase 7 Swing. Throughout Phase 7 Swing instruction you will find that I rely most heavily on those physical laws of motion that govern all objects that are set in motion. And, last but not least, Phase 7 Swing draws on my own empirical observations and what I've learned during the thousands of hours I've spent teaching students.

Yes, Phase 7 Swing very much presents my own brave, new world of golf instruction. Some of my professional colleagues have accused me of sometimes wandering too far into the weeds in my quest for new swing insights. Perhaps there is some justifiable evidence in their minds for branding me Radical Reeves. However, there is nothing radical about instruction that is rooted in science, tradition, careful observation and a painstaking assemblage of the revealed swing truths. Using my own home-grown insights and unique coaching techniques I've given thousands of hours of Phase 7 Swing instruction and produced what my students and all golfers are looking for: improved swings, more powerful ballstriking, consistent impact, better scores and great golf. The results of Phase 7 Swing speak volumes—Phase 7 Swing works.

To keep things simple, I've divided the book into three sections. In the first section, I explain the unique insights of the golf swing that Phase 7 Swing brings to the discussion. I also provide brief tutorials on how Phase 7 Swing adheres to the scientific laws of motion. The chapter, "Newton on the Tee," will build confidence in the simplified system of seven phases that make up Phase 7 Swing.

In section two, you will learn step-by-step how to master the seven phases. You will learn about the positions of IN and OUT, which are useful terms for reminding you where your hands and clubhead are placed along the swing plane in each individual phase, and how to run the all-important engine of the swing—the pivot. I have found that my students relate better to learning phases, which are dynamic, rather than positions, which are static. The golf swing is nothing but moving parts, so this idea makes sense. And it works. All that you need to do is learn the phases, follow directions and practice.

In section three, I help you apply Phase 7 Swing to some important shots such as the fade, draw, chip, and those involved in greenside bunker play with a simple "addition by subtraction" method of execution, and putting. Learning the correct ways of hitting these shots is critical to improving your scores and having fun on the golf course.

# A Guide to First Swings

My intent with this section on first swings is to give you a brief introduction to the seven phases of Phase 7 Swing and to duplicate a bit of the instruction you would receive in an initial one-on-one lesson with me, in other words, your "first swings." Later in chapters 5, 6 and 7, we'll return to assembling the seven phases in a more detailed, step-by-step approach. This Phase 7 Swing-Lite focuses on learning the meaning of terms such as plane angle and becoming more familiar with the terms, IN and OUT, which are shorthand for the proxim-

Select a club and address the ball. Set your feet slightly more than shoulder width apart and bend at the waist. Tilt the head slightly downward but keep the chin off the chest and eyes focused on the ball. Distribute your weight evenly, toe to heel, but favor a bit of downward pressure of the feet on the turf. If I were to place my finger on your sternum and push, you would not move. You would be solidly rooted and centered around the axis of your spine.

**IN**

**OUT**

**OUT**

**Phase 1**: At address, push down on the handle, set the wrists early and allow this to take the clubhead directly up. As the clubhead breaks from address, the pivot moves the club back and in. Phase 1 is an IN position, that is, the hands start along the imaginary plane angle farther from the target line than the clubhead.

**Phase 2:** Pivoting clockwise (to the right), allow the clubhead to rise up and around behind you, shaft mirroring the right forearm; place the hands closer to the target line along the plane angle, which is an OUT position. At the top of the upswing keep the left arm below the height of the shoulder line and the shaft over the right forearm. The toe-to-heel weight shift, the bending (of the left leg) and straightening (of the right leg), and pivot make it feel as if the body is moving downward (the famous Palmer squat?).

**Phase 3**: Complete the upswing/backswing pivot. Without pausing, reverse the pivot, turning counterclockwise around the axis of your spine. Begin the straightening of the left leg and the bending of the right leg, which gives the feeling that the body is being pushed up. This action ends in Phase 7. Allow the hands to react to the forward pivot, moving down and forward toward impact. The clubhead lags. This is an OUT position, that is, the hands are closer to the target line than the clubhead.

ity of the hands versus the clubhead in relation to the target line. Four distinct IN and three OUT positions function as the signature positions of each of the seven phases. If you take this instruction to your local practice facility for some hands-on repetition of the swing phases you will not only greatly accelerate your mastery of the mechanics of Phase 7 Swing but also deepen your appreciation of Phase 7 Swing's scientific roots that are explained later in the book. So follow along with the accompanying photographs and let's give it a go.

| IN | IN | OUT | IN |
| :---: | :---: | :---: | :---: |
|  |  |  |  |

**Phases 4** and **5**: These are consecutive IN positions—the clubhead is closer to the target line along the plane angle through and a short distance beyond impact just prior to the body pivot pulling the clubhead inside and away from the target line.

**Phase 6**: The hands and clubhead switch positions along the plane angle again, to an OUT position, that is, the hands are closer to the target line. Properly executed with a tight rotation and no loss of spine angle the hands and clubhead remain on the plane angle even though they're now behind the player on the reverse side of impact.

**Phase 7**: The final switch. The clubhead in the follow-through moves closer to the target line. To review, the phases of Phase 7 Swing are IN-OUT-OUT-IN-IN-OUT-IN when IN signals that the hands are farther from the target line along the plane angle and OUT signals that the hands are closer to the target line along the plane angle.

When fellow golfers ask you how you learned such a solid swing so quickly, or dropped so many strokes off your handicap, you can tell them about this book and point them in the direction of the nearest bookstore, or my website: www.phase7swing.com

In the meantime, it's straight ahead. Turn the page and start your own journey to a golf game of more powerful ballstriking . . . every time!

# PHASE 7 SWING

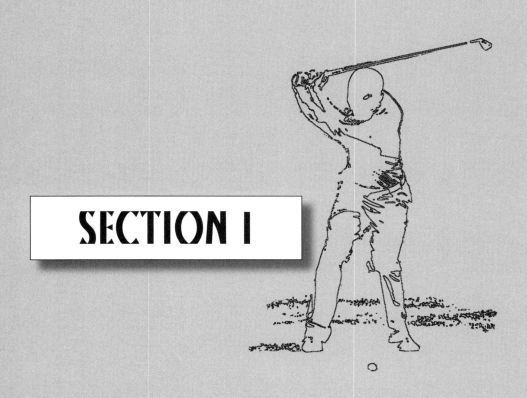

# SECTION 1

# CHAPTER 1

# Could It Be This Simple?

*The objective of the player is not to swing the club in a specified manner, nor to execute a series of complicated movements in a prescribed sequence, not to look pretty while he is doing it, but primarily and essentially to strike the ball with the head of the club so that the ball will perform according to his wishes.*

—*Bobby Jones*

The following acronym—*KISS: Keep it simple, stupid*—forms the guardrails of the journey you're about to take in swing instruction. Phase 7 Swing is simple in design and easy to learn. It is a perfect storm that combines time-tested tenets of the swing with powerful, new insights and paradigms.

Phase 7 Swing is contrarian in some ways on the surface—introducing a unique kinesthetic feel, for example—yet consistently in synch with the laws of physics and mechanics. To many, especially upon first encounter, Phase 7 Swing seems too simple. Some skeptics might think: "There's no way some cockamamie, one-size-fits-all swing system can help me!" And how can anyone synthesize the golf swing, a complicated athletic movement, by prescribing seven phases? My answer is that simple truth—like a naturally beautiful woman—is an eyeful to behold, and shows best when minimally adorned.

The enduring truths of the simple phases of Phase 7 Swing are like the classic lines that define the Ferrari sports car. Built for beauty and function, they create a classic rotational swing fueled by adherence to the laws of motion. You can rest assured that Phase 7 Swing will never wander off the reservation of solid science and spot-on swing instruction. With apologies to Hank Haney, this is the only golf lesson you'll ever need!

The fear of leading the consumer too far into the cosmos is well founded among innovators of all stripes and widespread in the world of new ideas, new processes, new products . . . well, new anything that you might imagine. A friend who develops new fragrances for perfumes cautioned me, "All the great new fragrances stem in some way or form from the classic Chanel No. 5 but they were gradual extensions, not radical departures." Message sent, message received. I embraced this caution as a useful and tempering thought as I began striking the keyboard. I promise you won't have to stand on your head or go through hell and high water to master Phase 7 Swing.

### *Some Things Borrowed From Master Teachers, Some Things Unique*

As a result of this friendly warning I came to think of my innovative Phase 7 Swing as a fresh, new scent born of both the familiar and new, a fallen fruit that settled a bit farther from the tree but not so far that its origin is untraceable. On these pages you will encounter thought-provoking perceptions and new terminology: however, Phase 7 Swing won't lead you down a dead-end trail. Phase 7 Swing will help you discover a simple system of learning the swing, a system that is rooted solidly not only in Newton's laws of motion but also in classic golf instruction and the traditional ideas of great instructors and legendary players of the past.

For example, fellow Brit Percy Boomer taught, among other essentials, that a player must "turn the body . . . without moving either way, in other words from a fixed pivot." Phase 7 Swing requires that the body pivot around a stationary axis—in this case, the spine—in executing the swing. The laws of motion confirm that a shifting axis leaks and greatly diminishes clubhead speed. Thus, Boomer's idea of "swinging in a barrel" is a building block of Phase 7 Swing instruction.

Phase 7 Swing in Phase 1 instruction tweaks and builds on PGA golf instructor Joe Dante's groundbreaking "magic move" of creating an early wrist break in the backswing (what I prefer to call the "upswing"), a concept first introduced in the 1960s in Dante's book, *The Four Magic Moves to Winning Golf*. Setting

## Great golfers are great strategists.

Great golfers are always great strategists. They not only manage their game (think Phase 7 Swing) but they also manage the course. The great player plans his shots for the entire hole and executes them in order. The not-so-great player plays shot after shot without considering the consequences. As Arnold Palmer once said, "One of my favorite things my father always said when I was a boy was, 'Golf is played 90 percent from your shoulders to the top of your head.' He used to love to say that. And he was right."

The basic goal of managing your game is picking the right target for each shot, and because the tee shot sets the tone for the hole, it might be the most important phase of managing your game. In most instances, if your predominant ball flight is from right to left, you should favor the left side of the tee box. If you usually curve the ball from left to right, you should tee the ball on the right side of most tee boxes. Regardless of which side of the tee box that you tee the ball, realize that a fairway bordered by trees on both sides, with no other hazards or obstacles, means the margin for error is reduced. Straight is more important than long. Consider a three-wood or other club that produces more accurate shots.

the wrists early, that is, before the hands rise above the waist in the backswing, not only helps place the swing on plane quicker in the upswing but also produces a storehouse of power that delivers a more explosive and powerful impact in the downswing. In addition, my Phase 1 instruction of Phase 7 Swing extends the understanding of the Homer Kelley/*The Golfing Machine* concept of loading the shaft early.

### Standing on the Shoulders of Nicklaus, Snead and Hogan

Jack Grout, the teacher of golf legend Jack Nicklaus, taught a concept very similar to an idea integral to Phase 7 Swing, what Grout called the ideal head position. Here is what he taught: "The ideal head position helps you maintain body balance while you swing and block any horizontal or vertical swaying." Phase 7 Swing incorporates this idea in each of its seven phases. Also note that the weight-controlling function of the ankles and feet during the swing, an understanding shared by Grout and Nicklaus, is also part of Phase 7 Swing instruction.

Phase 7 Swing challenges much of today's conventional golf instruction but it never goes where science cannot support its teachings.

The swing thoughts of the legends Ben Hogan and Sam Snead also shaped Phase 7 Swing. Hogan's critical insight—"you're heading for disaster if you thrust your arms up above the imaginary plane . . . that runs from the ball through the shoulders"—mirrors the positional goal of Phase 2 of Phase 7 Swing. Snead instructed that the left arm in the backswing should not rise above the nipple line of the chest, a move that mirrors Phase 2, which requires the left arm to stay below the right shoulder. *And so it goes throughout this book, the traditional and purest truths of the best teachers—all of them supported by empirical science—are melded with my ideas of putting the club and hands in seven basic positions to create your most efficient and consistent golf swing.*

Phase 7 Swing is what I call a *planar* model of motion. Planar simply means a two-dimensional motion that requires two coordinates to specify the respective positions of the hands and the clubhead. In Phase 7 Swing, I use the terms IN and OUT to identify in each phase these positions along the plane angle in relation to the ball.

Conventional golf instruction concerns itself with the single position of the clubhead. In this system, which is known as rectilinear, the clubhead can be likened to the tip of a spear. To gain momentum the spear must be hurled with the help of a pushing action of the lower body.

In contrast, using a planar model, the clubhead can be compared to the bladed head of a hatchet, which represents the first coordinate, and the hands gripping the handle, which represents the second coordinate. A hatchet gathers force when it exchanges positions with the handle, which is much how Phase 7 Swing works when the clubhead gathers force as it exchanges positions with the hands along the plane angle. Of course, it is nothing without an engine—the pivot—to effectively launch this exchange . . . more on this idea later.

Later in this book I will explain this concept—phase by phase—as I lead you through the exchange of positions of the hands and clubface relative to the target line, identifying the positions and clarifying any new terminology.

### Back Is Up

Here is an example, a swing concept that is captured with the new phrase, "back is up." Understand it, plant it deeply in your brain, own it, and you will be on your way to building a better swing using Phase 7 Swing principles.

## Perfect Practice Makes Perfect

Practice is the stuff of legend: Ben Hogan muttering that he dug his game out of the ground; Vijay Singh, a towel stuffed under his arm, hitting balls well into the twilight; or Gary Player not quitting his sand bunker practice till he holed three shots. Professionals practice not only long and hard but also with a purpose. Most of all, they practice the correct techniques.

Researchers have demonstrated that purposeful practice is the single, most significant factor distinguishing the best from the rest. One study of aspiring violinists showed that the best violinists had practiced more than 2,000 hours more than other accomplished—but not top-level—violinists. Yes, talent is important but practice makes the difference.

According to Matthew Syed in his bestselling book, *Bounce: The Myth of Talent and the Power of Practice*, an analysis of the top nine golfers of the twentieth century showed that they won their first international competition around twenty-five, which was, on average, more than ten years after they started golfing. Ten years, or 10,000 hours of practice, approximately 1,000 hours per year, appears to be the magic number for reaching performance excellence.

Jack Nicklaus knew that success sprung from purposeful practice: "Nobody—but nobody—has ever become really proficient at golf without practice, without doing a lot of thinking and then hitting a lot of shots. It isn't so much lack of talent; it's a lack of being able to repeat good shots consistently that frustrates most players. And the only answer to that is practice."

As Nicklaus said, the key to perfect practice is to think about the practice shot before hitting it. Never fire off shot after shot in rapid fire. This tactic shows lack of focus. Practice with a clear goal in mind. Pick a target and try to hit your shots to the target.

Leading PGA golf instructor Joseph Laurentino advised in his bestselling book, *The Negotiable Golf Swing: How to Improve Your Game Without Picture-Perfect Form*, that when on the practice tee use the following model for improving your shots:

1. Hit the ball.
2. Observe feedback, that is, the flight of the ball.
3. Make a diagnosis, that is, what did the club do?
4. Choose an element, such as the grip.

5. Make an adjustment, such as rotating the left hand.

6. Hit the ball to achieve desired result.

Sessions like this will help build better ballstriking, a correct tempo, improved timing, a workable setup and a higher level of consistency.

It's likely that you have a fraction of the time than that of a professional player to practice your game. A pro can spend three or four hours daily on the practice tee, both before and/or after rounds on the course. It is equally important, however, that you avoid practicing incorrect mechanics, thus ingraining a bad habit. Do this method and you will be on the road to ruinous golf. So the first step in perfect practicing is learning the right way to swing, the correct techniques of executing a shot or rolling a putt. Then you can be sure that every minute devoted to practicing will be well spent—and productive. You will improve and move closer to perfect play—pars, birdies and eagles—on the course.

When I ask my students on the lesson tee to grasp that "back is up" in the takeaway, not "low and slow as you brush the ground behind the ball," they sometimes recoil at this new way of perceiving this essential golf swing motion or, worst yet, silently withhold approval of the new terminology to describe it. However, they have the advantage of repeating this seemingly strange, new movement under my watchful eye until it becomes familiar and routine.

First they replace the swing thought of "low and slow" with "back is up." Then they match the movement with the thought; the clubhead comes up (Phase 1 of Phase 7 Swing) and is set comfortably "behind the ball," another new phrase that comes with a new meaning. And before long they own the phrase "back is up," that is, the body repeats the motion without a conscious reminder. Now they're on their way to constructing a consistently powerful swing. Repetition and muscle memory—coupled with consistent ball flight—make them not only Phase 7 Swing believers but also accomplished converts.

As the new phrase, "back is up," illustrates, Phase 7 Swing will teach you to think about the golf swing in new ways. This concept is healthy. Many roads, some less traveled, lead to golf's eternal verities. Here are two additional insights, two new ways of thinking about the swing:

1. The left wrist does not open or close the clubface—the pivot does
2. The left wrist does not rotate to the right in the backswing—the left wrist goes up, straight up.

Rest easy, mate. I assure you, I will explain these ideas more fully in Chapter 2. What you're about to learn, the seven phases of Phase 7 Swing, is not just some complicated, wild-hare golf swing system. As advertised, it's simple, as simple as two and two are four, as true as "what goes up must come down."

### *The Swing You Don't See—*
### *Seeing the Unseen in Phase 7 Swing*

Let's keep rolling. Here are two more morsels of what you will be digesting in later chapters. They are elements of what I call the *swing you don't see*:

1. The arms do not take the club back—the pivot does
2. The arms do not take the club up—the left wrist does.

I sense that you are now scratching your head, conjuring thoughts of ridicule.

Are you thinking that these ideas are absurd? No, not really—when closely scrutinized these assertions hold up as solid science applied to the golf swing. It's all very lovely, mate, and part of a simple seven-phase system of swinging the golf club. Please do not dismiss these swing ideas out of hand. Keep an open mind—Phase 7 Swing can help you. Phase 7 Swing can improve your ballstriking and raise the level of your overall game. So, if the arms do not take the club back, what does? Answer: the pivot!

### The Pivot Takes the Club Back

Phase 7 Swing holds that the pivot takes the club back, not the arms as conventional instruction advises. How do we know that the pivot takes the club back? You're thinking: The arms take the club back. Well, let's take a closer look. Try moving the club back along the ground—low and slow, as conventional golf instruction advises—without cocking or setting the wrists. Where does the clubhead go?

Back? Yes.

Back and up? No, not quite.

In fact, it goes back and back and farther back along a line on which you want to start the ball upon impact, that is, the target line, but it does not go up. From the very beginning of the backswing, you need to do something else to move the club up, around to the back (of your body, not back along the target line) and thus complete the backswing. What might that step be? Might it be something you don't readily see, something you don't consciously think about, especially when you're focusing on "low and slow?" It might be that you don't in fact need to take the club low and slow. And so it's fair to ask, "What exactly is this move that gets you ready to swing down, forward and through impact? What does it look like and what does it feel like?"

Like Cold War diplomats, we will trust but verify. My students benefit from the best of the past and the rest of the new, and so can you.

### Special Move—Performed Unconsciously

The move I'm referring to is a full flexing of the left

**1-1**. The pivot brings the clubhead up and behind you.

wrist toward your body, what is commonly recognized as an early setting of the wrists. This move consists of *a downward pushing of the wrist perpendicular to the target line (when executed as part of Phase 1 of Phase 7 Swing)—the left hand heel and the grip's end moving down, forcing the "business end" of the club, the clubhead, to move up, the left arm straightening while the right arm bends at the elbow.* Then, when you add a pivot—hips and core leading—to the right, the right hip and shoulder moving clockwise, the club goes up and back behind you.

Voila! *You don't see this part of the swing (normally, you don't even think about it).* It comes—naturally, if you will—with the body's pivot. It's there but your focus is usually elsewhere, perhaps keeping your eyes on the ball or feeling the movement of the clubhead "low and slow" along the turf in the takeaway.

There is stark contrast between the futility of storing power by a lateral "low and slow" takeaway versus the more powerful rotational loading of the swing in Phases 1 and 2 of Phase 7 Swing. More on this idea later but for now remember: 1. The former promotes a push of the right side on the downswing all the way to impact; 2. The latter promotes a pulling of the left side, a centripetal force that uses the mass of your rotating core to send the clubhead speeding through impact and beyond. Forgive me for getting a bit ahead of myself with this comparison, but this difference is so critical to understanding the efficacy of Phase 7 Swing that I just couldn't resist popping off about it before you've even been introduced formally to Phase 7 Swing.

### Radical Reeves—Not Really.
### Revelatory Reeves—Absolutely!

Some of you may have come across my videos on You-Tube or found me on the Internet while randomly surfing for golf instruction videos and such. I'm there in cyber-space in full force. I've even been called Radical Reeves for my adherence to Newtonian physics and my full-fledged embrace of its governance of the golf swing. This book is in great part about applying the laws of physics to the learning of the golf swing.

### Heeding the Laws of Motion of Sir Isaac Newton

Forewarned is forearmed. As we go forward on these pages we have a bit of science and math to learn as Sir Isaac Newton has some important things to say about how to hit a golf ball consistently. My goal, in part, is to show you how the understanding and application of Newton's laws of motion can facilitate, in short order, the mastery of the golf swing. Of course, my overriding goal is to introduce you to seven phases of the swing that can simplify its mastery.

### Let Yourself Go Out of Your Comfort Zone

I'm fully aware that you didn't pick up this book to expand your math and science horizons. When I first sat down at the keyboard I had to face a nagging fear that I might wander too far afield, that is, that my instruction would dwell too much on the science governing the swing than on how to develop a better golf swing. However, Phase 7 Swing does require a bit of intellectual stretching and learning when first studied in addition to a minimum level of kinesic discomfort when first attempted.

Readers of this book will also need to exhibit a bit of faith and patience. I know that learning the Phase 7 Swing can be done with or without a seasoned eye to assist. With the

**1-2**
ADDRESS

**1-4**
IN

**1-3**

**1-5**

# The
# PHASE 7
# SWING

Address—Phase 3

Phase 7 Swing **address position** (Photos 1-2 and 1-3) is standard: set up with feet slightly more than shoulder-width apart, weight evenly distributed, back and spine angled forward at 30 degrees, knees gently bent, arms hanging perpendicular to the ground. This is a position that is termed **IN**, that is, the hands are farther than the clubhead—along the swing plane—from the target line.

In **Phase 1** (Photos 1-4 and 1-5) push down firmly with the heel of the left hand (this step raises the clubhead) and take the club **up** while at the same time pivoting to the right, the left shoulder moving under the chin. This is also an **IN** position. The shaft of the club should follow the imaginary plane created by the right forearm; the shaft is apart but tracking the forearm. Immediately set the cocking of the wrists. The feeling of the right arm and wrist created by Phase 1 is similar to that of an angler preparing to cast a fly rod as the rod begins its rise overhead. While pivoting, pump the left leg forward but not so much that you lose balance or move off-center. Turn the hips, torso and shoulders. Remember, in Phase 7 Swing, **back is up**, not to the rear along the target line. **This motion is unique to Phase 7 Swing: The wrist cock brings the club up and the pivot takes the clubhead back.**

OUT

OUT

In **Phase 2**, set the shaft of the club directly over the right forearm as you complete the pivot. This is an **OUT** position, that is, the hands are closer to the target line than the clubhead. Raise the left arm no higher than shoulder height, preferably just below the shoulder (Photos 1-6 and 1-7). Keep the pressure on the shaft by extending the left wrist as far back (toward the right) as possible without losing control of the grip. Turn till your back is facing the target, left leg bending at knee toward the target line, center of head over and slightly behind the ball. *Note:* In completing Phase 2 you have put loft on the club (see position of clubhead at completion of the pivot).

In **Phase 3** (Photos 1-8 and 1-9)—another **OUT** position—start the forward downswing by dropping the arms (let gravity help build shaft and clubhead speed) and then forward alongside the right side of the torso and right hip. The right elbow is alongside the right hip as both move to initiate the accelerating momentum of the clubhead. The hip rotates around the axis of the spine and the elbow continues in Phases 4 and 5 to moving through and past the impact area, straightening just after the clubhead catches up to hands and arms at impact. The turning of the body is a center-seeking force, also known as a centripetal force, which creates the outer force, or centrifugal force, which propels the rapidly moving clubhead. In Phase 3, the clubhead starts to build its release by initially lagging behind, building momentum, and subsequently accumulating tremendous speed along its path to the ball.

COULD IT BE THIS SIMPLE

## The PHASE 7 SWING

Phase 4—Phase 7

In **Phases 4** and **5** (Photos 1-10, 1-11, 1-12 and 1-13)—both of these are **IN** positions, the hands are farther than the clubhead from the target line—keep turning fully through the pivot and moving the weight onto the left side with the left heel rooted firmly with the ground. Drive the right (rear) shoulder past the ball and around, as far your hips will allow. Stay over the ball, and allow the right arm to straighten after impact. Feel the surge of energy of the shaft's release as it propels the clubhead through the impact area. The striking of the ball is a violent deflection along the arc of the swing and the path of the clubhead. There is no conscious effort to hit the ball, only to swing the club forcefully—yet under control—as the energy passes along the shaft and into the clubhead as it speeds through the impact area.

OUT    IN

To properly execute **Phases 6** and **7 (**Photos 1-14, 1-15, 1-16 and 1-17), you must rotate the right shoulder past the point of impact while maintaining the spine angle for as long as possible. A loss of spine angle is natural in the follow-through and termination of the swing but the spine angle must be held in place as long as possible during Phases 1 through 5 so that all the stored energy passes through the impact area and down the line toward the target. Correctly done, you will feel as if you're staying over the ball longer than ever before. The sound of contact will be distinctly stronger, and ball flight will be longer and higher. Phase 6 is also where the top hand (right hand for a right-handed golfer) rolls over the top of the left hand—please, not anytime prior—as you move from an **OUT** position to the finish, an **IN** position.

latter, it just takes a bit longer. However, Phase 7 Swing is not alone in this regard. It has always been a challenge to take a book's golf instruction to the practice tee. Even Ben Hogan's classic, *Five Lessons: The Modern Fundamentals of Golf*, raised as many questions among neophyte golfers as it answered. So the message here is, "Stick with it." You won't be disappointed.

### Can Mastering Phase 7 Swing Really Be So Simple? I Think So.

First, understand that the golf swing takes place on a nearly flat two-dimensional plane that reclines at an angle up, back and toward the player, who acts as the center of the arc created by the on-plane swing. *In Phase 7 Swing, I represent the swing in seven simple phases, using the terms "IN" and "OUT" to remind the player where to position his hands along the plane angle in relation to the ball and intended ball flight.*

*When the hands are positioned along the plane angle farther than the clubhead is from the ball or intended line of flight, the phase is termed IN. When the hands are closer to the ball and the intended line of flight than the clubhead—again, each positioned along the plane angle— I term this phase OUT. Four IN positions and three OUT positions* exist in Phase 7 Swing. In each of the phases of Phase 7 Swing, the hands and clubhead switch positions, "IN" and "OUT" along the plane angle. The arms react, including raising and lowering the clubhead, to the pivoting or rotation of the hips and shoulders. Phase 7 Swing gets no more complicated than envisioning the plane angle, learning these phases, including the interplay between the body's rotating core and arms, and the respective positions of the clubhead and hands, that is, IN and OUT, along the plane angle.

### *Food for Thought—Phase 7 Swing*

Here are a few innovations of Phase 7 Swing. Contrary to years of conventional swing instruction, you will learn that the clubshaft need not rise above the shoulder in building an on-plane swing. Those who follow this swing path create a swing that mirrors the swing of the legendary Ben Hogan. Phase 7 Swing replicates the famous Hogan swing a whole lot more consistently than almost all other Hogan-derived swing instruction books.

Phase 7 Swing produces the most efficient swing in less time than any other instruction. You establish an individualized swing plane and then move the clubhead and hands along this plane through seven distinct phases and positions. Some of my beginner students have literally mastered the phases, the positions and the swing, in one lesson! There is no complexity, just seven phases to learn and replicate, a kind of follow-the-dots notion after learning the scientific rationale.

Phase 7 Swing has been stripped of the layers upon layers of mechanics that confound players and in the end fail to produce a powerful, repeatable swing they so desire. Phase 7 Swing delivers—you'll read more in ensu-

**1-18.** The clubshaft need not rise above the shoulders.

**1-19.** The clubhead rises and moves behind the player during the pivot.

ing chapters—a handful of new insights concerning the swing, including:

1. No need to shift plane angles—a source of power leakage

2. No need for a rearward tilting of the axis of the spine on the downswing—another source of power leakage

3. No backswing or forward swing—the body pivot around a fixed axis, the spine, looks after these motions

4. No active role of the arms—they're passive, letting the wrists take the club up and pivoting body takes it back and in; gravity takes the swing down and the pivoting body takes it out and forward

5. No lateral shift of body's weight—successive toe-to-heel and heel-to-toe weight shifts maintain the center of gravity and spine angle and eliminates excess lateral movement

6. No complicated terminology—instead, seven phases to learn and replicate.

### *Phase 7 Swing Cures Common Mistakes*

Phase 7 Swing, figuratively speaking, is a medicinal elixir for the myriad of ailments that afflict struggling golfers. Here is a smattering of the swing ills that you will cure.

1. Swaying off the ball/excessive body movement. One of the most common and most damaging swing ills is the weight shift that is too dramatic on the takeaway or backswing. Players get into trouble when the weight moves to the outside of the right leg. This action causes the entire body to move enough behind the ball that the bottom of the swing arc is also moved rearward, often as much as six to eight inches. When

**1-20**. Swaying off the ball is a ruinous fault.

**1-21**. A traditional pivot often moves the center of the swing rearward—a weak and precarious position for initiating the downswing

**1-22**. A Phase 7 Swing body pivot stays over the ball and leaks no power.

this situation happens, your axis for rotating is no longer centered. Phase 7 Swing develops a pivot that keeps the head and body over the ball and eliminates lateral movement. The latter causes all kinds of poor shots, including the dreaded chunk, or ballstrike that hits the turf two to three inches behind the ball. My students have learned that "the target is the ball." When you strike the ball properly, it flies to the target. There is no need to use "body English" or a body slide toward the target to send the ball straight and true.

2. Leaning out toward the target line. Some players tip or lean toward the ball during the swing, causing them to lose contact with the ground, and thus diminish an important source of the swing's power. This mistake also causes the ugly-as-sin shank as the hosel of the club moves out and over the target line at impact, sending the ball off to the right at a 45-degree angle. Phase 7 Swing teaches a toe-to-heel shifting of the weight that keeps the body centered around the axis (your spine) and prevents it from moving toward the target line. I like to remind my students, "You can hit it clean when there's no lean."

3. Reverse weight shift, commonly referred to as a re-

**1-23**. The reverse pivot—no way to generate power.

verse pivot. When the weight is flip-flopped, that is, the weight shifts into the front leg on the backswing and the weight shifts to the rear leg in the downswing, the result is a weak swing with its power left solely to upper body, arms and hands. Phase 7 Swing develops two key movements to prevent the reverse weight shift. The first is the centered axis, which establishes the angle of the torso and spine for pivoting to the right (backswing) and to the left (through swing). The second is the route of the left arm in the backswing—because it never rises above the right shoulder, the shoulders turn in arc that is more parallel to the ground and thus the body has little cause to tilt forward onto the front leg. Instead, the weight is loaded into the inside of the right leg with power-laden pressure applied to the ground and full extension of the left arm along the intended swing plane.

4. Casting from the top and coming over the top. When a player casts the club from the top or comes over the top, that is, he starts the swing by thrusting his right shoulder out toward the target line and swings mostly with his hands and not his lower body, he shuts off his source of power—the pivot. These faulty movements route the club outward as it starts its descent, which mainly produces a weak cut, slice or pull hook depending on the clubface position. Phase 7 Swing keeps your upper body quiet during the downswing. In Phase 3, the club drops while the body brings it forward with its pivot around the axis. This is a powerful move, as explained more fully in Chapter 7 in the explanation of Conservation of Angular Momentum.

5. Slapping the ball with the arms rather than turning

the body through the ball. This swing fault is a cousin to casting or coming over the top, as they fail to use the power source of the lower body. The power lies in your pivot, the lower body rotating around a fixed axis. The power is generated from the pressure of the feet pressing against the ground and the bending of the knees. Let your arms react to your pivot.

6. Hitting at the ball instead of swinging through the ball. Because Phase 7 Swing shows you how to create a powerful pivot, a source of centrifugal force that accelerates your clubhead to more than 100 mph, there is no need to think of "hitting the ball." Yes, the ball will be violently struck but only because it gets in the way of a powerful force. The collision of the clubhead with the ball—really, a deflection off the face of the club—is part of the swing's continuum. Although impact is where the rubber meets the road, it is not a destination. It is but a single dynamic point along the journey of Phase 7 Swing.

# CHAPTER 2

# The Power of the Left Wrist

*Understand that golf is neither a right-handed*
*nor a left-handed game, but a two-handed game.*
*—Ernest Jones*

Ernest Jones is correct. Golf is a two-handed game. It is also a two-wristed game, the right and left wrists each playing an important role in the swing (and when putting). However, I believe that the role of the left wrist holds the power to make or break a swing, especially the execution of the Phase 7 Swing.

The power of the left wrist is twofold. First, it controls the clubhead, including the very important squaring of the clubface at deflection, or moment of impact with the ball. Second, the left wrist is the final link in the left-arm swing chain that locks the entire left arm—a firm wrist with its back facing the target—from the shoulder down to the hands as the clubhead reaches impact in the forward swing. Let's take a closer look.

When I say that the left wrist controls the clubhead I am referring to how the clubface follows the bending or rotating of the left wrist joint. Try this action and see it for yourself. Grip a golf club and then remove your right hand. Now, roll your wrist to the right. What happens?

**2-1** and **2-2** . Rolling the wrists, two hands on the grip, opens (above left) and closes (above right) the face.

The face moves clockwise, the toe moving like the hands of a clock in a circle. Roll the wrist to the left and the face closes as it goes counterclockwise. Hinge your left wrist toward you—an element of Phase 1 of the Phase 7 Swing—and watch: The butt of the shaft moves down and the clubhead moves up.

This upward movement is the cocking of the left wrist that begins Phase 1.

As you move the club up you will feel the weight of the clubhead. This weight or gravitational pull begins to stress the shaft. In Chapter 5, I discuss stressing the shaft more completely but, suffice it to say, here the left

**2-3** thru **2-6** . As you move the club up you will feel the weight of the clubhead.

**2-7**. The left wrist aligns the shaft over the right forearm.

wrist is loading energy that will be released downstream in the swing sequence (Phases 3, 4, and 5). The left wrist holds the power to load the shaft, which it then releases during the body's forward rotation or pivot.

The left wrist performs another key movement in this early setting of the wrists. It places the shaft over the right forearm and the plane created by the right forearm as it folds at the elbow into the right side of the body. The left arm does not rise above the shoulder, thus the left wrist has positioned the shaft and clubhead at the top where it can be dropped and pulled through the impact area with no manipulation of the spine—no loss of the spine angle and no reverse C (a finish position in which the spine and lower body take the

**2-8**. As the right arm folds at the elbow into the right side of the body, keep the left arm from rising above the shoulders.

shape of a backward letter "C"). Remember: The left wrist sets all this action in motion by moving the shaft over the right forearm on the pivot to the right as the club swings up and never along the ground.

### Controls Power at Impact

Now let's take a look at how the left wrist locks down the power at impact and transfers the stored energy of the swing into the back of the ball. Top PGA teacher and The Golf Channel host Martin Hall said, "I can't think of anything worse to try to do with a golf club in your hands than 'accelerate and follow through.' Does the swing accelerate? Yes. What's making it accelerate? Gravity. And a force known as angular momentum—more on this term in Chapter 7 sidebar, Conservation of Angular Momentum, COAM. Is there a follow-through? Of course there is. Why? Because of the swing, because of momentum . . . If you think 'accelerate and follow-through' when you swing, then you are going to try to help momentum. Momentum doesn't need any help."

I agree with what Martin said but I think there is more to be learned about gravity, momentum and the role of the left wrist in the through swing. Yes, gravity does help. What feels heavy going up feels light going down.

Yes, momentum is building (more on this idea in Chapter 7 when I discuss Conservation of Angular Momentum) as the body pivots forward. In Phase 7 Swing you are using the mass of your body—via the tight (no lateral movement) pivot—to build and maintain a constant speed of body rotation. But the left wrist is also working hard to deliver a successful striking of the ball. It is holding the angle of the stressed shaft as the body pivots and the hands ride down and forward, clubhead lagging. And the left wrist is locking down at its flex point (in physics,

the fulcrum of the joint) at impact, keeping the back of the left wrist and hand facing the target. It is what I call the "load and lock" magic move of the left wrist.

This locking of the left wrist at impact not only squares the clubface but also keeps the right wrist from rolling over—counterclockwise—too soon and spoiling the ball strike.

**2-9**. The locking of the left wrist at impact keeps the chain of rising power intact at impact and beyond (shown).

## Linear and Rotational Energy

Physics 101 is in session! Today's topic—linear and rotational energy.

When a club comes in contact with a golf ball, it transfers two types of energy: linear, for distance, and rotational, for spin. Each hit generates a limited amount of energy, so if more energy goes to rotation, less is available for distance.

When a ball is hit dead on, pure backspin is imparted. Typical ball spin rates of elite players are 3,600 rpm when hitting with a 10-degree driver at a swing velocity of 134 mph, 7,200 rpm when hitting with a five-iron at a swing velocity of 105 mph and 10,800 rpm when hitting with a nine-iron at a swing velocity of 90 mph. The angled face of the club pinches against the ball and makes it rotate backward toward the club. For just a millisecond, the ball actually climbs up the face of the club. The grooves on the clubface help generate backspin because they increase the amount of friction between the ball and club. Conversely, wet conditions decrease friction and reduce backspin. A headwind increases backspin, while a tailwind decreases it.

Rotational forces generated by backspin increase the amount of lift experienced by a golf ball. Therefore, if a ball with backspin has the same trajectory as one without backspin, it will stay in the air longer. For example, if both trajectories have a height of sixty-five feet, a ball with backspin will stay in the air for six seconds; one without backspin for only four seconds. These two seconds can equate to as many as thirty yards on the course. A ball's rate of spin is partially dependent on the relationship between the ball's core and its cover. A ball having a harder core relative to its cover will spin faster.

Hitting the ball with an open clubface and a club path from out to in will cause the ball to spin from left to right. The ball will curve to the right or slice. Hitting the ball with a closed clubface and a club path from in to out will cause the ball to spin from right to left. The ball will curve to the left or hook.

## Coefficient of Restitution

Coefficient of Restitution (COR) of two colliding objects is a fractional value representing the ratio of speeds after and before an impact. For two objects to register a COR of zero, the objects would "stop" at the collision, not bouncing at all.

The coefficient of restitution entered the golf world when golf club manufacturers began making thin-faced drivers with a so-called "trampoline effect" that creates drives of a greater distance as a result of an extra bounce off the clubface.

When the club strikes the ball, it is deformed and flattened by the force of impact (balls with harder cores deform less than softer balls). The upper limit of COR permitted by golf's governing bodies is at 0.83; golf balls typically have a COR of about 0.78.

The coefficient of restitution of the ball varies between different types of balls. In general, a harder ball will travel further than a softer ball because it deforms less and will efficiently transfer more energy from club to ball. To obtain maximum distance in the drive, a ball must be selected that maximizes restitution for the club speed. If the chosen ball is too soft for the club speed, too much energy will be spent deforming the ball and not enough energy will be stored in the ball. Similarly, if the ball is too hard for the club speed, then the ball will not deform enough, and again, will not transfer adequate energy. It is important to choose a ball that matches the club speed.

Militarily speaking, the left wrist is both the control and command center and the firepower on the ground.

It is also true that the momentum that Hall described does not need a conscious thought "to accelerate" the clubhead. Rather, in Phase 7 Swing, you need to hold tight and turn hard. Because the rotating body mass is so great and the clubhead is relatively light in weight, the clubhead has what in physics is termed a low moment of inertia, or MOI. The MOI is a measure of the opposition a body (the clubhead) exhibits to its speed around an axis, which may or may not be fixed. The left wrist cocks the shaft over the right forearm, it rides gravity at the onset of the downswing, it holds the angle of shaft as it turns on the plane created by the right forearm, and it locks down at impact to deliver all the energy stored in the stressed clubshaft.

The left wrist leads you to the ball and flies your ball to the target.

The left wrist holds the power to make or break a swing.

# The Swing You Don't See

*Golf is a game of motion and rhythm, not position and mechanics.*

—*Martin Hall*

It's true, golf is a game of motion and rhythm. But we often miss seeing the elements of motion that make up a perfectly good golf swing.

In baseball, a pitcher leads with his elbow as he delivers the ball to the catcher. This essential part of the pitching arm's acceleration forward is unseen.

In tennis, a player rolls the wrist and top of the racket forward in hitting a topspin forehand shot. The rolling of the player's wrist and forehand is in plain sight but unseen. We see the sweep of the racket, a blur in real time, but not the essentials of the technique.

In Phase 7 Swing we also encounter what I term "the swing you don't see." In your mind's eye, picture doing the following. From the address position, the shaft resting along an inclined plane, cock the left wrist. This motion will take the club up, moving the shaft from an incline (slant) to horizontal to incline to vertical and back to incline. In Phase 7 Swing terminology we call the address and Phase 1, that is, the cocking of the wrist, an IN posi-

**3-1** thru **3-3**. The "swing you don't see" is the raising of the clubhead up (above, left and center) and around back (above, right), which is masked by the turning of the body in the pivot.

tion in which the clubhead is closer to the ball along the inclined plane.

Without a body pivot, this move resembles the initial stage of casting a fly rod when the angler prepares to make the cast. However, in golf, when you add a pivot the same movement appears in the mind's eye—paradoxically—as if the shaft remained at the incline position as it moved back, up, and in—or what I call "behind the ball."

As the swing moves from Phase 1 to Phase 2—the switching from an IN position to an OUT position in our Phase 7 Swing system—we don't see the shaft moving from incline to horizontal to incline to vertical and back to incline. It is "as advertised"—the swing you don't see. But there is more to what doesn't meet the eye.

### Width, or Getting Behind the Ball— Straight Up in Phase 1 Provides Width in Phase 2

Here is an additional element of the swing that you perform unconsciously and, thus, do not see

**3-4**. Width, or getting behind the ball, is achieved by taking the club straight up and around back.

for what it really is. This element is camouflaged by the body's pivoting (around back to the right in Phases 1 and 2 and then forward to the left in Phases 3 through 7). This unseen element of the swing is what is commonly referred to as **width**, or **getting behind the ball**. In Phase 7 Swing, width, or getting behind the ball, is achieved paradoxically. You produce width, an objective of Phase 2, by taking the club straight up and back in Phase 1.

The left arm straightens when the club is set at the top of the backswing. This straightening is the true measure of the radius of the arc you've created in preparing for the downswing

**3-5** thru **3-7**. Phase 1 combines a narrow, linear distance rearward with an abrupt 90-degrees rise of the clubhead to set the club at the top, a position that does not raise the clubshaft above the shoulders.

## Phase Connotes Dynamic Movement, Not a Fixed Position

Please note that I use the term "phase," which connotes dynamism or movement, and not the term "position," which infers a static or fixed place along the motion-rhythm continuum of the swing. As explained more fully in Chapter 1, *Phase 7 Swing is a system of continuous motion and rhythm segmented into seven checkpoints—four IN locations of the hands vs. the clubhead and three OUT locations— along the way.* The eyes can see much of this continuous motion but they don't see all, and what they do see is always one's individual perception, not what a slow-motion camera would reveal as the empirical reality. We don't always see but in our mind's eye we always can know.

## Three Types of Practicing

Practicing can take at least three forms: 1. warm-up practice, 2. target practice and 3. swing practice. Practicing your swing is very different than warm-up practice and target practice. In learning Phase 7 Swing, or any new swing system, you should spend more time in the early stages practicing your swing. Swing practice allows you to bite off one-by-one each of the seven phases of Phase 7 Swing, focus on training your body to learn the kinesthetic feel of these phases, and then combine the phases away from the competitive juices that stir when on the course.

Swing practice allows you to revisit your new swing fundamentals without concerns for consistent ball flight. With the aid of a mirror or a practice buddy it allows you to stop and look at your positions, to get a mental image of the correct technique and mechanics. Learning a new swing pattern takes repetition. Some researchers say that it take upwards of 1,500 repetitions of a new athletic movement before the conscious brain turns off and the unconscious one takes over. Getting the movement right from the beginning brings meaning to the saying, "Practice doesn't make perfect; perfect practice makes perfect."

Errors pertaining to swing fundamentals are responsible for nearly every error a golfer can make. So it makes great sense to work on fundamentals at the beginning of the learning of a new swing system and to devote time periodically throughout the golf season to return to the practice tee and work on your swing mechanics.

Do not try any of this practice when playing a round. Play golf when you're competing for low scores. Practice when you're trying to ingrain good mechanics. Leave your swing thoughts on the practice tee and while you're on the course use your playing thoughts.

and approach to impact. This radius is the measure of the width.

What you don't see in Phase 1 of Phase 7 Swing is that when you bring the club straight up (*See Photos 3-5, 3-6 and 3-7*)—an action that creates a narrow, not a wide linear distance between the clubhead and the ball—***you are actually setting the club's arc as wide as possible when*** *you finally stop pivoting: Phase 2.* This idea is a paradox. The less linear/more upward that the movement is in Phase 1, the more behind the ball you will be in Phase 2, which terminates at the top of the club's ascent up and behind your right shoulder.

This reality exists because "behind the ball"—where you take the club to achieve width of the swing arc or the greatest radius of the swing—is behind your head, not to the rear along the target line. *When you are pushing the clubhead low and slow rearward along and parallel to the target line you are—to borrow a phrase—merely "traveling hopefully"; when you bring the clubhead straight up and use the early wrist cock "you've arrived." The swing you don't see is what gets you there.*

Traditional golf instructors advocate creating width (wide swing arc) by pushing the club low along the top of the grass and along the target line as long as possible and

> The width you're trying to create is actually behind you.

**3-8.** Behind the ball is actually behind the pivoting shoulders, not to the rear of the ball along the ground and target line. This is the strongest launch position of the golf swing.

then taking it up and around back. ***In reality, the width you're trying to create is actually behind you, not to the rear along the target line.*** Because you're pivoting while sweeping the club away from the back of the ball it's impossible to keep expanding width without bringing the hands up and the clubhead around to the back.

So why go "low and slow" when you can get to your destination and achieve the width you desire by taking the clubhead straight up? ***You can get behind the ball by cocking the left wrist, stretching the left arm, placing the shaft over the right forearm and stressing the shaft all the way to the top.***

### When Do I Get to Just Grip It and Rip It?

Why is it important to rethink where "behind the ball" really is in the backswing? After all, you might be thinking: Is it really important to know exactly what I'm seeing in my mind's eye versus what's documented on the video replays as I make my backswing? Am I raising the clubhead straight up over the right shoulder (Phases 1 and 2)? Can I see this motion? Do I need to see this motion to make a good swing? Can I focus solely on setting the club at the top, regardless of how I got it there, and still make a good swing?

Good questions, mate! In the end, a blend of skepticism and curiosity makes for a more committed student and convert. Read on and you will know the answers. Be prepared to become a believer in the simple, verifiable mechanics that make up Phase 7 Swing.

### Behind the Ball — How to Get There

First, words are important. They convey specific meanings. When you are instructed to take the club "back," your reaction is to move the clubhead low and slow along

> The pivot takes the club away from the ball and directly to the true position of "behind the ball."

the target line. But the term or word "back" captures only a part of the movement that prepares the club for the downswing and through swing. To do this part, you must do more than go "back" or make a backswing. You must get "behind the ball," which requires that you take the clubhead up. This part happens, of course, in Phase 2 of Phase 7 Swing when you add a pivot. Ben Hogan knew this point, and he taught it in his classic swing book, *Five Lessons: The Modern Fundamentals of Golf,* when he wrote, "The action of the arms is motivated by the movement of the body [the pivot], and the hands consciously do nothing but maintain a firm grip on the club."

In Phase 1 you get behind the ball by taking the clubhead straight up. Thus, getting behind the ball is not a matter of simply taking the club back. In traditional golf instruction, taking the club back is, at best, the initial step of getting behind the ball. It is true that in tradi-

## Create a Swing Station

A helpful action you can take to make your swing practice focused and productive is to create a swing station on the ground, using your clubs. Lay one club on the ground just outside the ball and parallel to your target line. Lay another club along your toes, to use as a reference in positioning your feet, hips and shoulders. The two clubs should be parallel. Then take a third club and use it to mark ball position for whatever club you are swinging. You can position this third club perpendicular to the other two, and you can put it either between your legs or outside the club you are using to mark the target line.

Replicate the different lies you'd encounter in a typical round. Take a tip that Arnold Palmer learned form his dad: Alternating shots that have good and bad lies, from balls resting in rough, thin and thick, and balls lying on the short grass. For example, position the ball in a divot and hit it to targets that vary by ten yards, say from eighty yards through 130 yards, the all-important approach shots. Learn how to strike a ball with the lower half of your clubface, and observe what happens when you do. Memorize the trajectory and the carry versus roll components of such shots. Practice like Palmer's dad and watch your scores drop and your confidence rise.

**3-9**. Swaying off the ball—a weak and precarious position for launching the downswing.

tional golf instruction that first step can ultimately lead to a position of "behind the ball" but not as powerful or as simply as moving from IN (Phase 1) to OUT (Phase 2).

"Behind the ball" (*Photo 3-8*) is fully achieved at the terminus of the backswing, the point at which the left arm is extended, the wrists are cocked, and the body is ready to move into the downswing and through swing, the point at which the club, shaft and its head are most effectively placed for delivering the most powerful striking of the ball.

To summarize, you are behind the ball at the conclusion of Phase 1 just as you are transitioning to Phase 2. At this juncture, you have created the widest radius of the arc of the downswing, initiated in Phase 2.

### Decrease the Chance of Moving Too Far Off the Ball

Which is more useful? Mastering how to brush the clubhead atop the grass or setting the club and getting it straightaway into the perfect launch position to do some serious business? The latter, of course, is what's going to allow you to strike the ball more powerfully and play

better golf. The former, a commonly practiced mechanical movement of getting you into the proper position at the top, increases the chances of moving the center of your body rearward.

This reality is because the simple act of pushing the club straight back along the target line promotes the shot-killing flaw of moving laterally (*Photo 3-9*), and, in the process, shifting

**3-10**. In Phase 7 Swing when one leg is bending the other is straightening—you're eliminating lateral motion and creating a powerful rotary movement that generates and transfers speed and energy to the clubhead.

## The Tomahawk Effect ... Add the Pivot and You Won't See It

What is the tomahawk effect? Well, imagine a swing with no pivot, a motion of simply picking up the clubhead by cocking the wrists and raising it over your right shoulder (*Photos 3-11 thru 3-13*). If you wanted to strike the ball from this raised-arm position you'd swing directly down on the ball and release the clubhead by uncocking the wrists. It would be the same as chopping or striking the ball with a tomahawk. No sweep into the backside of the ball, no long arc created by the body's pivoting—only a vertical blow delivered with a powerful downward force.

Well, if you add the pivot (*Photos 3-14 and 3-15*) to this tomahawk action, you will create the golf swing. The downward force is coupled with a sweeping centrifugal force provided by the body's pivoting to the left around a fixed axis (your spine) and when the deflection occurs between the clubhead and ball, off goes the ball into the air. Lovely, mate! You've struck the ball with a tomahawk effect that you did not see.

**3-11** thru **3-13**. The tomahawk motion. **3-14** and **3-15**. Add a pivot and the tomahawk motion becomes part of the overall ballstriking motion that combines the torso's rotary motion with the downward, chopping motion of the tomahawk to create a forward swing.

weight, which was evenly distributed at address, shifts to the inside and heel of the right foot. You move the weight away from the toes and ball of the right foot toward the heel. You feel as if you're moving slightly down, what many players, including Arnold Palmer, described as the feeling of squatting on a stool. What you don't see,

## No More Fat Shots

Here's another practice tip that can help you improve the consistency of your ballstriking. Draw a fifteen- to twenty-inch line in the turf that is perpendicular to your target line. Before you hit each ball place it just forward of the line. Swing and make sure that your divot always begins forward of the line. This setup will help you eliminate striking the turf behind the ball before hitting the ball. Use this mental reminder or "swing key" as your last thought before taking the club away: "Firm right side, weight on my inside right heel." Voila—no more fat shots!

**3-16**. Divots that start at the line perpendicular to the target line demonstrate correct ballstriking—the divots are forward of the line. Divots made behind the line are poor strikes and usually result in weak shots that do not carry the intended distance.

of course, is the weight shifting initially to the rear (to a braced right leg) and then to the front leg and foot without any lateral sliding of the body off center (the bottom of your swing arc remains intact).

This movement happens

Phase 1

Phase 5

because the pumping or flexing of the knees effectively shifts the weight back and forth while keeping the body centered over the ball. Phase 7 Swing is the ultimate system for keeping the weight centered and producing a powerful centrifugal force in the forward pivot.

In the body's pivot to the right, the rear or right leg straightens almost totally as the front leg bends deeply (knee moving toward the target line, not rearward and

Phase 2

Phase 3

Phase 4

Phase 6

Phase 7

## Phase 7...Above

This sequence of the Phase 7 Swing demonstrates the secret of pure ballstriking. The golfer moves the hands along the plane angle and mirrors this plane angle with the clubshaft. Look closely at Phase 4 and Phase 6 to see that the tight, rotary pivot has allowed the golfer to generate clubhead maximum speed—while staying over the ball throughout—yet kept the clubshaft on the same plane angle when entering (Phase 3 ) and exiting the impact area (Phase 6). No power was leaked.

parallel to the target line). This movement allows for a full pivot to the right without a change in the spine angle or a slide laterally off the ball. In the pivot that starts the downswing and through swing, the right leg bends, driving toward the target as the left leg straightens and locks at the knee, allowing the pivot to continue, bringing the club through impact (Phases 3, 4, and 5) and around to the left and back (Phases 6 and 7).

# Newton on the Tee

*The golfer generates power through sequential movements of force through the larger muscle groups into the smaller muscles and an accelerated motion in order to gain the highest clubhead speed at the moment of impact.*
—*Taras V. Kochno, M.D., Sports Medicine and Rehabilitation International*

Because the "sequential movements of force," or mechanics, of a functional golf swing are rooted in the empirical world of physics, it is helpful for the average golfer to gain at least a cursory understanding of the observations of Sir Isaac Newton, a physicist whose laws of classical mechanics first explained motion in the seventeenth century. It is also helpful to know and understand other scientific principles that significantly govern the swing. For our purposes, however, we are limiting the discussion to Newton. Professional golf instructors should study further the role of science in the golf swing so that they can bring this knowledge to the lesson tee and provide quality instruction to their students.

I know you didn't buy this book to master physics (you

## Newton on the Tee

Sir Isaac Newton's three laws of motion form the basis for modern physics. His laws apply to golf. In a capsule, here's how:

### Newton's First Law of Motion

Newton's First Law says that an object in motion will remain in motion until it is acted upon by an outside force. We know that a golf ball moves when a force is applied to it. We also know that a golf ball always stops, even it is merely rolling down a fairway unimpeded. Therefore, it can be concluded that outside forces are always acting on an object.

Many outside forces act on a golf ball that prevent it from moving in its original direction forever. Gravity pulls the ball toward the earth, preventing it from traveling on the straight-line path it took when the club struck the ball. Air resistance, a form of friction, slows the ball's velocity as it travels through the air. Once a golf ball hits the ground again, friction is increased because a grassy or sandy surface creates much more friction with the ball than air.

### Newton's Second Law of Motion

Newton Second Law of Motion can be stated with this equation:

$$Force = Mass \times Acceleration$$

Mass is the amount of matter an object has per unit of time that it is traveling. Force is the product of acceleration and mass. In simpler terms, if a really big thing is moving at you with that same acceleration, the big thing is going to hurt a heck of lot more because its force is much greater.

Newton's Second Law prevails throughout golf. When a golfer chooses a wood to hit off the tee, he will probably choose the driver if he's looking for the greatest distance possible that he can achieve with his swing. The clubhead mass of the driver is greater than that of all other golf clubs. Even if he swings with the same club acceleration as with the other clubs, the driver should theoretically outdrive all other clubs because of the extra force that is imparted on the ball at the moment of impact with the club.

An alternative way to increase distance on a drive is by swinging faster.

If a golfer swings faster than usual and meets the ball squarely, extra force will be created because the acceleration of the ball's mass has been increased. Using the techniques of Phase 7 Swing, you can swing faster by moving your body quicker when pivoting. The increased speed of your rotation—that is, the pivot—feeds momentum down the shaft to the clubhead by way of Conservation of Angular Momentum (see Chapter 7). Accelerating the movement of the big muscles of the torso and upper body—by using pressure against the ground—is a more consistent way to increase speed, and thus shot distance, because you keep the hands quiet through impact. The wrists square the clubface at impact without additional, conscious manipulation.

### Newton's Third Law of Motion

Newton's Third Law of Motion states that for every reaction, there is an equal and opposite reaction. When a force is applied to the inside back of a golf ball with a club by swinging (the action), the ball rockets down the fairway (the reaction). If a golfer does not meet the ball squarely with his club, he produces a reaction that may be undesirable. A slice, where the ball fades off to the right for a right-handed player or to the left for a left-handed player, is caused by a golfer not meeting the ball squarely. In a slice, the golfer makes uneven contact with the ball, imparting a tight spin on the ball that is similar to that of a curveball thrown by a baseball pitcher.

A hook is similar to the slice, except that the uneven contact results in the ball spinning in the opposite direction (to the right for a lefty, to the left for a righty). A hook acts in a similar manner as to when a baseball hitter "pulls the ball," except that there is a much more vicious sideward spin on the ball in a hook, taking it far off course from its original straight-line path to the target.

want to master Phase 7 Swing), so our discussion will be brief and devoid of technical gobbledygook.

A small bite of Newton-Lite is all that is necessary to help us understand and master the mechanics of the golf swing. Understanding how the world of physics applies to the golf swing will provide not only the analytical tools to assess one's performance but also a solid base for making any changes that might improve one's play. To develop Phase 7 Swing, I consulted over several years with not only the world's best golf instructors but also world-class physicists, mathematicians and kinesiologists. Each gave me valuable insights in their respective fields for building the Phase 7 Swing system.

So let's step up to the tee and find out what insights Newton has contributed to our understanding of the golf swing. Of Newton's three laws of motion, Newton's Third Law is especially important for the mastery of Phase 7 Swing. This principle explains how we initiate the kinetic chain that launches those 300-yard drives. Although Newton's first and second laws also apply to the golf swing, we will not discuss them in detail here. [If you want to know more, you can read the accompanying sidebar or explore Newton's laws in greater depth by looking up his laws at http://www.physicsclassroom.com/class/newtlaws.]

### Newton's Third Law of Motion

According to Newton's Third Law, for every action force there is an equal (in size) and opposite (in direction) reaction force. Forces always come in pairs— known as "action-reaction force pairs." Identifying and describing action-reaction force pairs is a simple matter of identifying the two interacting objects

**4-1**. To apply Newton's Third Law, push down with your feet on the turf.

**4-2** and **4-3**. The ground powers the golf swing. For every action there is an equal and opposite action: The feet push down on the turf as the turf exerts pressure upward (Photo 4-2). Friction increases till the opposing forces are released when downward pressure of the feet and legs is diminished and/or ceased (Photo 4-3).

and making two statements describing who is pushing on whom and in what direction. For example, consider a baseball approaching the plate and colliding with the barrel of the batter's bat.

Now consider gravity and the downward pressure created by the muscles of the legs as the feet push into the turf while at address and during the golf swing (*Photo 4-1*). You create this pressure through the bending and straightening of the legs at the knees.

The turf or ground, aided by friction, pushes upward. The pair of forces, each pushing in opposite directions, causes the feet to remain firmly planted in the sod.

The golf swing begins with this firm foundation, the feet set shoulder width or slightly wider apart. The feet function much like the anchoring roots of a tree—the tree's roots keep it in place and the feet, when properly engaged, prevent lateral movement of the body. ***The bending and straightening of the legs at the knees create the rotary motion that keeps the body over the ball and prevents drifting.***

During the pivot of the swing the feet push down hard on the turf, allowing the hips to swivel or turn around the fixed axis of the spine. The ground pushes upward, friction keeping the feet in place, the head over the ball and the torso centered between the feet. *See Photos 4-2 and 4-3.*

The result of these powerful opposing forces is the formation of a rock-solid platform for the body's pivot.

The core of the body, which controls this pivot, harnesses the power of the body's mass as it turns around the spine. The magnitude of this power is raised by increasing the downward pressure of the feet and gravity because—as Newton's Third Law predicts—it produces an equal force pushing upward.

The significant force needed to rotate the body's core is greatly assisted by a stable base. There is no wobble, drift or lateral slide. And the rotation of this large mass of the body takes place along what is known as the body's transverse plane, which dissects the body along a plane that is perpendicular to the angle of the spine. Thus, when a player tilts his spine an approximate 30 degrees at address—and maintains this spine angle throughout the swing—he makes the most powerful swing. All of this movement begins with the paired forces at work during address as described in Newton's Third Law.

This kinetic sequence requires dynamic balance to prevent a lateral leakage of the power and a stationary head to avoid moving the bottom of the swing rearward.

> The core of the body harnesses the power of the body's mass as it turns around the spine.

### Kinetic Chain

Kinetic energy is the energy of a body with respect to its motion. The several motions of the golf swing form a chain, which I call the kinetic chain. What happens during the upswing (backswing) and downswing (forward swing)—two important elements of the pivot's kinetic chain—creates two distinct and opposite feelings: 1. When the body is pivoting around to the back, the right shoulder disappearing behind the body as it rotates clockwise, the weight shift from front to back feels as if you're moving down; 2. When the body is pivoting forward, that is, when the right shoulder moves counterclockwise to the front and forward toward the target, the back-to-front weight shift feels as if you're moving up.

I am certain that you've seen some players literally lift themselves up and off the ground just after impact. Going airborne is the result of Newton's Third Law: For every action force there is an equal (in size) and opposite (in direction) reaction force. The downward pressure or force exerted by your core and legs through your feet is released upward when friction can no longer hold your feet in place. And remember, Newton's Third Law is also at work in the arc of the swing: When the club is thrown down at the ball, an equal force is reacting upward. If you would like to see this idea demonstrated, look up on YouTube the swings of Joe Miller, 2010 RE/MAX World Long Drive Champion who won with a 414-yard drive. In a recent coaching session with Miller, we have worked on keeping the kinetic chain intact through impact so that all force is captured and applied to the ballstrike. The results are more power and longer distance.

### Stripe It Like the Sultan of Swat

When students ask me how I determined the shape of the swing, I tell them, "It came from source." This is not a

## How to Make a Good Pivot

In this chapter we've been learning about forming the platform for a good pivot, which begins with a solid and rooted address position. So, what exactly is a good pivot? First, the upper spine must be as straight as possible. For every degree that your spine rounds from the bottom of the shoulder blades to the back of the neck you lose 1½ degrees of rotation. This is a serious flaw, as Phase 7 Swing depends on a full and powerful pivot.

**4-4**. The spine at address should approach an angle of 90 degrees to the shaft of the club.

The spine at address needs to be set up at an angle that approaches 90 degrees, or perpendicular to the shaft of the club (*Photo 4-4*). The rotation of the shoulders also needs to be 90 degrees, or perpendicular to the spine during the backswing and through the swing. This movement allows for a rotation along the body's transverse plane. The lower body must remain stable and support the coiling of the torso and rotation of the shoulders.

Do not focus on the shoulder turn. Instead, focus on the bending and straightening of the legs at the knees. When turning back or away from the ball, straighten the right leg and bend the left leg, the knee moving toward the target line and not toward the right knee (or back along a line parallel to the target line). When turning forward, straighten the left leg and bend the right knee, turning it to face the target as the weight is released to the left side at impact and beyond (Phases 4, 5 and 6 of Phase 7 Swing).

When turning the right hip around your back and away from the ball, be careful—some players turn too much. The result is that the knees do not work properly, causing the lower body to break down and lose balance. Players who turn too much forget that the body has to drive onto the front leg—which is straightening during the through swing and at impact—and unwind through the ball. Video footage of an overturn in the backswing shows the club slowing down, not accelerating, at impact. The acceleration of the clubhead must come from the lower body driving and the torso pivoting around the inside of the front leg (Phases 4, 5 and 6).

The movement in Phase 2 eliminates the swing flaw of solely turning the shoulders too far around back in the backswing because the clubhead goes directly up and allows the player to get behind the ball without any excessive raising of the club (above the right shoulder). Thus, Phase 2 of Phase 7 Swing virtually eliminates a problem before it can develop.

The next move is to exchange the body weight that is pressing down on the turf. Shift this weight from the rear foot, where it has been concentrated on the inside of the sole, arch and heel, to the front foot, rolling it onto the outside and at the finish, to the toes (*Photos 4-5 and 4-6*). Unwind the upper body, bringing the arms and hands down alongside the body and firing the clubhead through the hitting zone.

Your entire body—but especially the legs and torso—controls the amount of the turn that takes place in the swing. It provides a certain amount of resistance that restricts the rotation of your hips and shoulders. If you should concentrate on turning any single part, that is, the shoulders or the right hip, you risk getting out of synchronization. Don't overly think about the pivot, except to focus on the pumping or flexing action of the knees. We should heed the advice of legendary teacher Harvey Penick: "The turn is a natural movement of the body . . . you will read and hear many complex instructions about the turn, but not from me."

**4-5** and **4-6**. The feet exert downward pressure throughout the swing and release it in Phase 6 and Phase 7—after impact—of Phase 7 Swing.

**4-7**. Baseball's legendary slugger Babe Ruth, who was known to hit the golf ball a long way, used a rotational swing to amass his 714 home runs and consistent tape-measure shots, on and off the baseball diamond. The Babe's swing literally spun him like a top, his rear shoulder replacing his front shoulder upon the finish of his swing. Ruth trusted his big muscles of his core when he swung, knowing that he could control them more easily. He fired them in sequence, lower body leading, to generate the bat and clubhead speed necessary for power and longer ball flight. This technique of "big muscles of the body's core leading the way" is an important element of Phase 7 Swing.

flip answer. What I mean is that the swing evolved from science and math, from the laws that govern the material world, especially motion. I simply observed what these disciplines revealed, and then synthesized these scientific revelations with seven simple phases so that golf's most powerful swing can be mastered more easily by the average golfer.

"Source" revealed a swing motion that is nearly 100 percent rotational. I say "near 100 percent" because man is not a machine and only a machine (think Iron Byron) can replicate a motion perfectly over and over again. In baseball, the immortal Babe Ruth, the legendary Sultan of Swat, used a rotational swing that literally spun this prodigious home run hitter into the ground. He used the pressure of his feet to tap into the kinetic chain that ran from his feet, up through his stabilizing legs and rotating core to create a strong pulling action by his front arm. This motion produced a powerful swing that created tremendous speed of the bat head. Home runs followed, just like the way Phase 7 Swing yields 300-yard drives.

Contrast the Babe's purely rotational swing with the flowing weight-shift swing of Seattle Mariners outfielder, Ichiro Suzuki. Suzuki's swing is to baseball what Curtis Strange and similar lateral-shift players are to golf. Without perfect timing, the gliding back and forth while swinging cannot be consistently harnessed. Even when a glider's swing is perfectly timed, it seldom delivers the same amount of speed at impact as a purely rotational swing. The power leakage is too much to overcome.

So stick with "source" and you can stripe it every time.

### Flamingo Drill

Here's a simple drill that will help train you to keep the clubshaft over the right forearm during the swing. Stand on your left leg, right leg folded behind you like a flamingo. Grasp the club with the right hand only and a slightly choked grip. This setup takes the left wrist out of our practice drill. Address the ball, right hand only on the handle.

Lift the club straight up over the right forearm, what I call "mirroring the right forearm," and then pivot clockwise till the right shoulder is behind you (approximately 90 degrees from its position at address). Pause momentarily, and pivot forward or counterclockwise to initiate a strike at the ball. As you pivot and bring the club down you should feel the clubhead building momentum. The pivot will sweep the clubhead down and through the impact area toward the ball, causing a deflection off the face of the club—the ballstrike! Even when you have taken the tomahawk action of the left wrist out of the upswing and downswing, you have effectively swept down and through the ball by keeping the shaft over the right forearm (the only one in use for this drill). Who said that a one-legged, one winged bird couldn't give flight to a golf ball?

In applying Phase 7 Swing principles to the swing of Joe Miller, 2010 RE/MAX World Long Drive Champion, the goal was to capture all of the power that was generated through the kinetic chain, that is, to apply all—or as close to 100% as humanly possible—of the swing's force to the ballstrike.

No lateral-movement leakage of the body during the upswing (takeaway), minimal sidespin of the ball during its flight and dead, solid contact with the clubhead. Newton's Third Law—for every action force there is an equal (in size) and opposite (in direction) reaction force set the parameters of Miller's swing mechanics, the same forces that govern the different phases of Phase 7 Swing.

In short, we followed and adopted the natural laws of movement , nothing more, nothing less. Sir Isaac Newton, on the lesson tee in absentia, was our guide.

Phase 7 Swing minimizes the forward knee (left knee) "chasing" after the rear (or right) knee, that is, moving rearward

# ..World Long Drive Champion

and closing the gap between them. Rather, the left knee moves away from the center of the body toward the target line, as correctly demonstrated in the third frame above, thus allowing for a tight, rotational pivot. The result is an absolute maximum accumulation of clubhead momentum and application of power.

In this sequence, Miller's core—his back, abdominal and leg muscles—combine to create downward pressure through his feet. The turf or ground pushes back with equal force. Miller's downward throw of the clubhead at the ball creates an upward force of equal measure.

These opposing forces—applied powerfully within the constraints of a tight, rotary pivot—release after impact—that is, after the ball is on its way. Downward pressure of the feet diminishes, the friction no longer holds the heel of the right foot in place, as the club moves past impact, up and around to the back.

# SECTION II

5

# Start Stressing the Shaft—
# Phases 1 and 2

*You get rewarded at the bottom of the club*
*by what you do at the top end.*
                                    *—Jerry Barber*

Golfer Jerry Barber offered this insight long before the inception of Phase 7 Swing but his words are especially true in learning Phases 1 and 2 of Phase 7 Swing. For example, when you push down on the handle of the club to initiate Phase 1, thus reversing the position of the hands from IN to OUT (at Phase 2), the "bottom of the club" rises to its proper position at the top of the backswing.

The rewards are threefold:

1. Maximum cocking of the wrists
2. Fullest stressing of the shaft
3. Proper lofting of the club

Upon completing Phase 2, one end of the club—the handle—has placed the other end of the club—the head—in position to execute a powerful, consistent swing. More rewards await in the forward swing and at impact.

### Back is Up, Back is Not Low and Slow
The first two phases of Phase 7 Swing switch the posi-

**5-1** thru **5-3**. Address, Phase 1 and Phase 2—from an IN position to an OUT position along the plane angle.

tion of the hands and clubhead, from IN to OUT, along the inclined plane (determined by the angle of the shaft in relation to the ground). Refer to *Photos 5-1 thru 5-3* to see these phases. To correctly initiate a Phase 7 Swing, you need to set aside what you have learned about creating width in the takeaway. Conventional golf instruction calls for the creation of width in the backswing with a low and slow takeaway of the club along a line that is parallel to the target line accompanied by a full extension of the arms. This movement starts the clubhead parallel to the target line for up to a foot or so and then moves inside and up as the body pivots.

Unfortunately, creating width with a conventional "low and slow" takeaway often causes a lateral movement "off the ball," that is, a swaying to the rear that moves the bottom of your swing arc to a spot that is behind the ball. Without a downswing adjustment, a conscious shift forward toward the target of the entire body (even super coordinated athletes don't do it consistently), the result is a fat shot, that is, a swing that strikes the turf behind the ball, or a thin shot, that is, a shot that is deflected off the lowest grooves of the clubface or the bottom edge. The practice of keeping the head as stationary as possible, advocated by many great teachers and players—among them the legendary Jack Nicklaus—is designed to promote a rotary movement in the backswing and downswing and thus avoid miss-hitting the ball, either fat or thin.

Here is the good news—Phases 1 and 2 of Phase 7 Swing do not direct you to create width in the takeaway. In contrast, Phases 1 and 2 require that you bring the clubhead straight up immediately—not back and up gradually—while making a strong pivoting of the hips and turning of the shoulders. Let's find out where the top of the backswing is and see exactly what happens when we follow Phase 1 and Phase 2 movements.

> The constant cocking of the left wrist allows the grooves of the clubface to look at the sky.

### Phase 1—Cocking the Wrists Early

Address the ball, slightly bent at the waist, feet slightly more than shoulder-width apart. Start Phase 1 of the swing by pushing down on the end of the grip with the outside of the left hand. This procedure raises the clubhead, straightens the left arm and cocks the wrists up-

**5-4**. Neutral grip.   **5-5**. Strong grip.   **5-6**. Weak grip.

## Establish Rhythm in Pre-round Warm-up

When you warm up before playing a round the objective is to prepare your body to play. Warm-up practice won't guarantee that you will play the greatest round of your life, but it does guarantee that you will play the first couple of holes much better than if you did not warm up. In addition, warm-up practice will enable you to shift your mental focus away from the details of your everyday life and toward the prospects of enjoying four hours playing golf in fresh air and bright sun among friends.

We asked Ben Crenshaw to give us some insights concerning his approach to warming up before a round of golf, and here is what he said:

"When I begin my pre-round warm-up routine, I'm usually looking to establish my rhythm and tempo for the day. I'm trying to get my muscles loose and get a feel for my motion that day and how fast or slow things are moving and maybe get a grasp of my timing.

"That's all I do for the first twenty-five balls or so I hit because, as all golfers know, you feel different every day. For example, if your hands don't feel quite right on the club, you've got to spend a little time finding a comfortable grip pressure. I pay attention to ball contact and where it's going, but I'm focused more on tempo and balance.

"I find it helpful to start out with my short irons, my wedges. The shorter swing motion is less complicated and a little easier to get a feel for. Because you're trying to get your feel for the day, try to keep things simple."

Note that Gentle Ben is not working on his swing or looking for a breakthrough key. He's taking the golf swing he currently owns and simply warming it up. The time for fixing is not just prior to a round.

ward. The wrist motion is similar to that experienced when casting a fly rod from overhead or flinging a hatchet into a tree. If you have trouble making this movement, check your grip. A neutral or strong grip plays well with Phase 7 Swing but a grip that is too weak can make it difficult. [Note: a weak grip is one in which one knuckle of the left hand is showing and four knuckles of the back of

**5-7**. The motion of setting the wrist, that is, flexing it as you bring the shaft up and back, thus mirroring the right forearm, is similar to that experienced when casting a fly rod from overhead.

the right hand are showing (player's view); a strong grip is one in which four knuckles of the left hand (rotated to the right) are showing and no knuckles of the right hand are showing (player's view). A neutral grip is somewhere in between. A neutral or strong left hand on the grip is easier to cock than a weak left hand.]

The downward push of the left hand raises the clubhead, thus creating an early setting or cocking of the wrists and puts loft on the club (more on this idea below). Hold this early cocking or setting of the wrists as you turn the right hip back and away from the ball. Keep turning the hips until the left shoulder moves under the chin. The successful completion of Phases 1 and 2 depends on a full pivot or rotation of the hips and shoulders.

The cocking of the left wrist in Phase 1, which keeps the shaft in alignment with the plane of the right forearm, stresses the shaft and readies itself for the whip-like acceleration of the clubhead that will be produced by the all-powerful lag in the through swing.

### Weight Distribution

While the shoulders and hips rotate, here is what's going on with the distribution of your weight. The weight moves toward the heel of the right foot as the right knee is straightening. [*See Photo 5-8*, which shows the right leg straightening about 90 percent

**5-8**. The left knee bending allows the hips to rotate around the right hip joint.

with a slight bend at the knee.] This step allows the hips to rotate around the right hip joint and keeps your weight from rolling over onto the outside of the right foot, a no-no. Imagine a small area of the inside of the right foot upon which you apply downward pressure as you rotate around the right hip joint. This pressure on the ground enables you to maximize the power that is released from the uncoiling of the hips in the downswing. With this solid connection to the ground you can more easily create the lag that accelerates the clubhead through the impact zone. This downward pressure of the right foot is released naturally at impact as the weight is moved forward onto the left leg and to the left foot.

In the takeaway or upswing, that is, Phase 1 and Phase 2 respectively, the left knee moves toward the toes and the target line. As you complete the backswing or takeaway, keep the front knee from chasing the right knee because this rearward motion will cause you to move behind the ball, another no-no. Do not raise the left arm above the right shoulder.

**5-9** thru **5-11**. The clubshaft aligns over the right forearm. It follows the path of the cocking wrist.

## Know the Distances When Laying Up and Planning an Approach Shot

Ben Hogan elevated the practice of game management to a science. When he won the 1953 British Open at Carnoustie, a course he'd never seen before, he spent days prior to the tournament just walking the course without his clubs. Sometimes he walked holes from green to tee in order to gain a new perspective of the hole.

The latter practice paid dividends when Hogan needed to decide how to play his layup and approach shots. He knew exactly how far his shots needed to carry when he faced a hazard that guarded a green. And when he chose to layup short of a hazard he made sure that he did not hit the ball too close to the hazard—a bad bounce could put his ball in the hazard. Hogan chose a distance from which he felt comfortable making a full shot and played his approach accordingly. He also knew the best angle to attack the green and thus played to the spot on the course that provided this angle of approach.

When you are laying up short of a hazard you need to know two distances: the distance between you and the hazard and the distance between you and the hole. Then do the math. As a general rule of thumb, it is advisable to layup approximately fifteen yards short of the hazard. Consider carry and roll in this equation, and, of course, the firmness of the playing surface. Play these shots like the pros. Pick an approach-shot yardage that is to your liking, that is, a distance from the target from which you feel great confidence in executing a distance-controlled shot. Perhaps you prefer hitting a 110-yard pitching wedge to a ninety-yard sand wedge. Hit your approach to 110 yards, pull out your pitching wedge and knock it close.

In Phase 2, the clubshaft aligns over the right forearm. *See Photos 5-9, 5-10, and 5-11.* It follows the path of the cocking wrist. Think again of the fly rod analogy; the right forearm supports the weight of the shaft. Gravity is temporarily neutralized—the cocking supports the shaft over the right forearm. If you permit the shaft to wander, such as rising too far above the forearm (you will be copying the backswings of Bubba Watson or Jack Nicklaus, who said he "wants his hands to go as high as possible"—we do not!), you will need to manipulate your posture during the downswing and through swing.

Specifically, if the hands go high above the shoulder you must tilt the axis or spine away from the target in order to put loft on the club in the through swing. This movement puts loft on the club but also adds a pushing action of the body's entire right side through the impact area, which causes you to leak power. The Phase 7 Swing calls for a rotation, what amounts to pulling action—a more powerful move. It keeps you over the ball and driving through it, not tilting the body backward to make room for the club's approach to the ball.

Phase 7 Swing also harnesses gravity as an accelerant to the clubhead's speed. You pull with the rotating hips, get your left hip out of the way at impact and the belly facing the target as the hands pass the front left leg . . . all of these motions in a synchronized split-second of coordinated ballstriking as the clubhead comes flying through the impact zone.

### Put Loft on the Clubface

The constant cocking of the left wrist in Phases 1 and 2 allows the grooves of the clubface to "look at" the sky. Loft is now on the clubface (*Photo 5-12*) and you're now ready to access—not fight—gravity when the club drops into the swing slot that is part of Phase

**5-12**. The constant cocking of the left wrist allow the clubhead's grooves to face skyward.

3. This clubface-skyward position will guarantee maximum height of your ball flight, that is, a trajectory equal to the respective degrees of loft of the particular iron or wood. You will not hit another smother hook or pulled hook. Worst case shot as you're mastering the Phase 7 Swing? Perhaps the high fade. More on how to adjust to this result in the next chapter.

### First Swings—A Beginner's Drill

Here's a simple drill that will help you get off to a good start in learning Phases 1 and 2. It calls for an emphasis on the pumping action or flexing of the left leg at the knee and rotation of the core. The efficacy of Phase 7 Swing resides in the mastering of a rotary swing around a fixed axis (the spine), so it's important to focus in the very beginning on turning or pivoting without moving off-center. After addressing the ball and taking the club up, extend the left knee out and toward the imaginary target line (drawn from the ball to the target). Straighten the right leg as much as possible (if you were holding an athletic position—knees slightly bent—lose it).

Unfortunately, creating width with a conventional "low and slow" takeaway often creates a lateral movement off the ball.

Next, turn the right shoulder in, or around to the back, away from the imaginary target line in a clockwise motion. When the right shoulder is turned approximately 90 degrees, stop the leg action. This position is akin to an archer's position of drawing his bow and taking aim with the arrow. Your core, legs and shoulders have created muscular tension. Your feet are pressing into the ground, creating more force that will be released milliseconds beyond impact. Most importantly, you are still centered—you have not moved laterally behind the ball—along a line parallel to the target line.

Take this drill to the practice tee by repeating this leg

action in slow motion prior to each shot. It will keep you from allowing the left knee to "chase" the right knee, which causes a swaying off the ball, and it will accelerate your ingraining of the totally centered pivot needed to successfully execute shots using the Phase 7 Swing methods.

# 6

# May the Force Be With You — Phases 3, 4, and 5

*The hips initiate the downswing. They are the pivotal element in the chain reaction. Starting them first and moving them correctly—this one action practically makes the downswing.*

*—Ben Hogan*

I like to tell my students that, in golf instruction, "terminology can let you down," that is, it can create images in the mind that inhibit the mastering of the golf swing. For example, in understanding Phases 3, 4 and 5 of the Phase 7 Swing I do not use the terms "backswing" and "forward swing." Instead, I substitute the terms upswing and downswing.

Why? Because the pivoting of the body, when done properly, looks after the backswing and the forward swing. I teach my students to master how to take the club up and down and how to make the body rotate properly. This motion will safely take the clubhead through the hitting area and completely avoid the perils of terminology that can ensnarl your swing.

This idea may seem like a bit of nitpicking but it's not. Let me explain. I believe that consistency is attained and power is achieved when the number of swing elements that must be learned are minimized, and when the number of body movements can be simplified. Thus, I've identified a mere seven positions of the hands and clubhead for learning Phase 7 Swing. I have not denied the existence of the so-called backswing and forward swing. Rather, I have assigned them silent roles in the swing, and chosen not to emphasize their mastery. They are simply a creation of the rotary motion of the hips and shoulders—the pivot.

I want my students to master a pivot that is rotary as close to 100 percent as possible, a ballstriking path that is a pulling—not a pushing—motion through the hitting

## Centrifugal Pulling Action

In his book, *Lowdown from the Lesson Tee*, fellow teaching pro and Top 100 Golf Magazine Instructor David Glenz offers some insight into the critical relationship between the pivot and the through swing, from the dropping of the club to initiating it (Phase 3) to the point beyond impact (Phase 7). Glenz correctly debunked the misconception that "the left arm controls the swing."

I agree with Glenz's assertion that pulling down with your left arm, if strictly followed without assistance and some kind of coordination with the rest of the body, will shutdown the centrifugal force that propels the clubhead. That's because the lower body initiates the swing. The arms never go first and they never work alone.

If the left arm works alone at any time during the swing, that is, if it is not part of a sequence of motions, as this idea unfortunately suggests, you cannot build clubhead speed. And without clubhead speed, you're left with no power to strike the ball.

Picture a baseball batter swinging at a pitch without the hips opening and the torso unwinding—this motion occurs when an off-speed (slower) pitch fools the batter. This action produces a weak swing, initiated and area. And I want my students to avoid as much as possible any lateral motion because this error is the leading cause of a power loss and inconsistent ballstriking (fat, thin, topped, bladed—you name it). The terminology of Phase 7 Swing will not let you down. It will lift you up to a better game of golf.

### The Arms Do Nothing

I know what you're thinking: "No way 'the arms do nothing' in the swing." Again, in building a Phase 7 Swing we want to pivot, stay over the ball from start to finish, and deliver the most energy and power at impact. Re-

completed by the hands and arms only. Missing is the all-important pivot that I believe is the motor that drives the swing—in baseball and in golf.

Yes, the flailing batter's lead arm (the left arm for a right-handed batter) would gradually straighten just beyond the point of contact as would occur in a correctly executed swing. But without the lower-body platform that allows the batter to pivot, the bat would transmit very little energy to the ball. In fact, a major league fastball at 95 mph would likely knock the bat from the batter's hand. Everything is wrong with this picture. There is no speed of the barrelhead, minimal transfer of energy to the ball upon contact and absolutely no chance of knocking the ball beyond the infielders.

In the golf swing, you suffer similar consequences when you pull down or forward with the left arm without coordinating this movement with the coiling action of the leg, hips and torso (Phase 2). You need more than the arm pulling the head of the club forward or down. You need the big muscles of the legs and torso to turn the body and create the centrifugal speed that builds in the forward-moving clubhead. You need the uncoiling of the back and side muscles of the torso to create this centrifugal pulling action. The arms, hands and clubhead are propelled to high speed by centrifugal force. When applied to the ball with a squared clubface and following the target line, the ball will fly straight and true.

member, we want to avoid lateral movement, any kind of other non-rotary movement, such as rising up or changing the spine angle at impact, which leaks power. So here's what I mean when I say that "the arms do nothing" in the swing.

The wrists in Phase 1 take the club up—remember there is no backswing, only a taking of the club up from address. The pivoting of the body in Phase 2 takes the club back and in, that is, sets the club at the top, a position in Phase 7 Swing that does not move the left arm above the right shoulder (a Hogan-esque position). Gravity takes the club down (*Photos 6-1, 6-2 and 6-3*), Phase 3, and the pivot takes it out to the ball, Phase 4, and forward, Phase 5 (*Photos 6-4, 6-5, 6-6, 6-7, 6-8 and 6-9*).

In Phase 7 Swing, we do not pay any conscious attention to what the arms are doing. We take the club up with the wrists and let the big muscles, legs and core unwind as we bring the club down into the impact zone. The arms

> We want to avoid lateral movement—any kind of non-rotary movement.

**6-1** thru **6-3**. Gravity takes the club down.

**6-4** thru **6-6**. The body's pivot takes the club forward to the ball.

go along for the ride, never leaving the plane on which they began

Newcomers to golf who were former athletes, dancers, martial arts practitioners—those who have learned how

**6-7** thru **6-9**. In Phase 7 Swing the golfer has the unique sensation of staying over the ball throughout the swing. The sound at impact is noticeably different—louder and more robust.

**6-10** thru **6-15**. When approaching the ball and through impact Phase 7 Swing eliminates lateral movement, the golf swing's most damaging fault. The spine does not tilt away from the target to allow room for the arms to swing under the shoulders. Instead, the spine firmly sets up as an axis for a freewheeling swing that allows for the fullest application of power. With Phase 7 Swing you will strike it more solid and hit it longer.

to control their body in athletic movement—learn Phase 7 Swing easier because their physical platform for delivering the clubhead is more stable than that of the average student. If you can control your body and maintain superior balance you can master golf by way of Phase 7 Swing faster than any other method.

### In Phase 3, the Hands Are in OUT Position Along the Plane Angle

In Phase 3, the hands are in an OUT position along the plane angle, or closer to the target line or ball. The left wrist is retaining the angle, which holds the loading of the shaft and creates the lag necessary for maximum power at impact. *See Photos 6-10, 6-11, and 6-12.* The body is pivoting, the left knee is straightening, the right knee is bending and the weight on the right foot is shifting from the inside heel toward the toe. Gravity helps drop the club down while the pivot brings it forward. There is no linear action of the body, that is, no tilting of the spine away from the target in the effort to drop the club into the impact zone. *See Photos 6-13, 6-14, and 6-15.*

The conscious thoughts in Phase 3 should be riveted on the uncoiling and the eyes must be looking directly at the inside-back of the ball. If you are correctly positioned as you come into Phase 4, an IN position—and devoid of lateral shifting—you will feel more directly over the ball than ever before. Johnny Miller might say you're "trapping the ball," that is, getting a downward strike flush on the inside-back of the ball that compresses the ball fully on the clubface at the absolute bottom of the swing arc. No energy is lost, and impact is solid. When you first master this swing, you will hear a more robust sound at impact, a distinctive crack of titanium colliding with dimpled urethane elastomer. The sound is as sweet as a door closing on a luxury Rolls Royce.

## Thoughts to Consider When Playing from the Tee

Here are a few pointers when considering your tee shot. First, remember that a tee shot is not always hit with the driver. A shot from the tee should be taken with the club that gives you the greatest chance of success. It is not always the biggest dog in the hunt, so don't always reach for the driver.

1. If, on a hole that doglegs, you think you can hit the ball through the fairway with your driver, do not hit your driver. For the most part, doglegs require only two straight shots: one to the point where the bend is, and the next one to the green. Few doglegs are so abrupt or so gradual that it helps to curve the ball around the bend. Just play it straight.

2. Except for expert players, it is seldom a good idea to choose a line that requires you to carry a tree or trees to bite off some of a dog leg. Remember: The closer the tree is, the less likely you are to carry it.

3. If you are faced with a forced carry off the tee, think carefully. Very seldom does a forced carry over water require you to carry the entire body of water. Unless a course is poorly designed, a target area in the fairway usually exists that allows shorter hitters to play the hole. Always remember: When you play a bold line, the ball is more likely to be offline as its distance from you increases. That last little bit you try to bite off is at the same point where your ball is running out of steam and curving most dramatically. So allow for a shot that is less ambitious than a career shot. Plan on a shot where the path gets you over the hazard safely, not on one that bites off the most yardage.

### *In Phase 4, the Hands Are in an IN Position*

In Phase 4 the left wrist is uncocking and releasing the load of the shaft. The left hip has pivoted around to the left, allowing the hands to ride alongside the right hip in an IN position. The club, which keeps its loft, strikes the ball at the bottom of the arc, creating a divot that begins slightly in front of the ball. If you have rotated the hips properly and thus eliminated any lateral movement, there should be no difficulty in staying over the ball throughout the downward swing and impact. The feeling should be a pulling, not a pushing, of the club through the impact zone. Your weight shifts to the left side as the right side drives through and then past the impact zone.

Legendary golfer Byron Nelson described the motion of what I call Phase 4 of the Phase 7 Swing as follows: "When entering the hitting area, the left hand and arm are pulling the clubhead. It is this action which gives you the full clubhead speed." I totally agree. Nelson was admired, and copied, for the maximum pressure he applied to the ball. He stayed over the ball and rotated as well as any of the pure ballstrikers that the game of golf has seen.

In Phase 7 Swing, we do not pay any conscious attention to what the arms are doing.

### *In Phase 5, the Hands Remain in an IN Position — A Key Movement*

In Phase 5, the hands remain in an IN position while the clubface maintains loft. The weight of the right foot moves onto the toes, right leg bending at the knee. The left leg straightens and the head stays over—not in front or behind—the impact point. Maintain a constant spine angle throughout Phases 3, 4 and 5. This setup will maximize the force applied to the ball and avoid the ballstrikes that produce a variety of offline and weak shots.

A properly executed Phase 5 actually extends impact beyond the point of deflection, that is, when the face of the club first strikes the ball. The ball actually goes off on a tangent to the path of the clubhead. Picture a child jumping off a merry-go-round that is spinning at great speed. The child is flung out and forward while the merry-go-round continues spinning.

**6-16**, **6-17** and **6-18**. In order to achieve full impact a golfer must swing through the ball. In Phase 7 Swing, the magic number is Phase 5 because it makes Phase 4—impact—disappear.

The arc of the spinning merry-go-round is similar to the path of the clubhead. The rate of speed does not decrease at impact. Rather, it continues at the same rate, or in some cases or with some swings, at an accelerating rate. But it does not slow down prior to impact, at impact or slightly beyond impact. It keeps moving just like a merry-go-round. The ball flies off in the direction of the club's path along the target line.

What I'm emphasizing here is: In order to achieve full impact, *a golfer must not swing AT the ball but THROUGH the ball*. This idea is not specific exclusively to Phase 7 Swing but it is crucial to any successful striking of the ball and to generating maximum distance.

Given the mastery of this technique, you will feel that this ballstriking feels almost effortless (picture Rory McIlroy's fluid movement through impact and beyond). *Maximum forward rotation of the body is the key to creating an effective Phase 5.* We

## Always Hit Shots to a Target—It's the Way Golf is Played

Golf is played by hitting one shot after another at a target. Targets can be specific sides of a fairway, a layup area short of a hazard or the green itself, including the area surrounding the pin. Practice your game on the range by hitting shots at targets.

Start with targets close to you. If the practice area has flags or "greens," use them as your targets. If it does not, pick out an area where you want to land the ball. Stop after each shot and go through your pre-shot routine, selecting your target and intermediate target, getting the clubface lined up properly and stepping into the shot properly.

One way to maintain your interest level is to change targets for every shot you hit. This strategy will prevent your practice outing from turning into a mindless slugfest because it more closely resembles what happens during a round of golf.

An excellent way to target practice, and another way of keeping things interesting, is to "play a round" right there on the practice tee. Place your bag nearby and mentally place yourself on the first tee of a course with which you are very familiar. After clearly seeing the hole and establishing a target for the tee shot, pull the club you would use to play the shot, and play a teed ball just as you would if you were actually on the course. Because you know the course well, you will be able to determine the outcome of your tee shot. If you think it would be in the fairway, then play the type of shot you would play from the fairway. If you think it would have ended up in the rough, play the type of shot you would play from the rough.

If you think you hit it into the trees, punch out. You can and should make this drill more fun by deliberating over each shot just as you would on the course, that is, consider the lie, wind and club selection.

When you are doing target practice, do not worry too much about the your swing. Focus on your routine and the flight of the ball.

call Phase 5 the "Magic Number" because it makes Phase 4—impact—disappear.

### *Perfect Impact is a Down-the-Target-Line Collision Between the Clubface and the Ball*

Here is a simple technique for building a powerful swing while eliminating the tendency of "hitting the ball" or, worse yet, "hitting at the ball," instead of the desired striking of the ball as a matter of the ball getting in the way of your clubhead at the bottom of its swing arc. When you move through Phase 4 and Phase 5, purposely miss the ball toward the inside, that is, take a swing path that is an inch or two closer to your feet. Strike the turf and continue through Phases 5, 6 and 7. The mastering of this technique will prevent you from hitting at the ball, a swing that actually slows the swing speed at impact. By practicing a swing that misses the ball, you will learn the correct feeling of constant acceleration through and be-yond impact. When you subsequently change your path to actually strike the ball, the impact (Phase 4) will be a force-laden collision with the ball. You will not lose speed

**6-19** and **6-20**. When practicing the Phase 7 Swing miss the ball toward the inside (closest to your feet). This helps to promote a pulling action and minimize a pushing action.

at impact and you will apply maximum power to the inside-back of the ball.

### No Gimmicks, No Contrived Drills—
### Just Seven Phases

I am often asked by my students for drills that they can take to the practice tee between lessons. At one time or another I tried them all, from tennis rackets to ice hockey sticks to basketballs pinned between the knees to ribbons tied to the clubheads. For my money, they are all rubbish, just a bunch of detours on the road to better golf. "Rubbish" might seem an assessment that is a bit harsh but what I've learned is that it's better to focus on learning how to execute the seven phases of Phase 7 Swing. These phases embody the science and art of the swing, capture the essence of consistent ballstriking and absolutely guarantee improvement with their mastery. The road to a better golf swing is not paved with hinged golf clubs, water buckets, aluminum ladders, ironing boards, garbage can lids or water hoses. Learn the phases of Phase 7 Swing, master them with diligent practice and you will build the world-class swing and better game of golf that you are striving to obtain.

# The Swing Is Not Over Till It's Over—Phases 6 and 7

*I think it pays to have the feeling that you are accelerating the club through the ball and out on into the follow-through . . . if you don't think of accelerating through impact, you'll probably decelerate a lot earlier.*

*—Jack Nicklaus*

In his book, *Golf My Way*, legendary golfer Jack Nicklaus cautioned readers against decelerating the club when it arrives at, moves through and passes beyond impact. These parts of the swing correspond to Phases 4 and 5 of the Phase 7 Swing system. With the execution of a proper Phase 1—the early cocking of the wrists—Phase 7 Swing practitioners will set the stage for the clubhead's acceleration on the downswing by stressing the shaft and loading the clubhead.

As with almost any sequence of swing motions, the correct execution of phases downstream, such as Phases 6 and 7, depends on the mastering of phases upstream. In this case, when Phases 1 through 5 of Phase 7 Swing are correctly executed, the successful completion of the successive phases, 6 and 7, is almost always assured.

To reinforce the idea of constant or accelerating speed through impact, Nicklaus **advocates that you feel as if you are accelerating the club at, during and beyond impact.** This mental key is extremely useful because high-speed photography has shown that the hands actually slow down near the point of impact despite our efforts to speed them up. The good news, however, is that this slowing of the hands does little to slow the speed of the clubhead, provided the golfer has held the angle of the Phase 1 cocked wrist entirely through Phase 3 (and thus not leaked speed and power by "hitting from the top," that is, throwing the head of the club at the ball instead of leading with the hands). The explosive power generated by the release of the clubhead that is lagging behind the hands in the downswing is explained by a phenomenon known as the **Conservation of Angular Momentum** (COAM).

> The correct execution of phases downstream depend on the mastering of phases upstream.

### Phase 6—
### An OUT Position Along the
### Plane Angle of the Swing

In Phase 6—when the ball is gone and the club is turning up and away from the target line and around the front and left side of the body—you position the hands in an OUT position along the plane angle. That is, the hands are closer to the target line and the clubhead is farther away on the same plane angle. *See Photos 7-1, 7-2 and 7-3.*

In Phase 6, loft is no longer on the clubface, as the top hand and arm roll over the left arm. The toe of the clubface tumbles counterclockwise over the heel, thus closing the face as the club moves to the left around the body and away from the target line. The weight of the right foot moves from heel to toe while the weight on the left foot rolls onto the left side of the foot toward the heel.

The right leg is bending at the knee while the left leg straightens.

No lateral shift of the body occurs, only a rotary action, a turning around the spine. When viewed down the line (from the rear), the angle of the clubshaft in Phase 6 replicates the angle of the club at the top of the backswing (Phase 2) and the arc of approach in the downswing (Phase 3). The angle of the spine is constant.

Most importantly, the pivot continues fully with the left hip rotating around to the left and back. A full and complete pivot—rotation of the hips and torso—is the key to successfully executing Phase 6. When the hips turn, the shoulders will follow, thus allowing the clubhead to release fully, that is, create an arc forward (after) of impact that is as wide as the arc created behind (prior to) impact. As Nicklaus sought, the fully rotating pivot maintains the speed of the hands and clubhead and helps the club deliver the most energy to the inside-back of the ball when struck by the clubface.

You should feel more that the club is being pulled through and beyond impact into the follow-through,

## What is Conservation of Angular Momentum (COAM)?

Phase 7 Swing is a practical application of the science of physics, specifically the rotation around an axis, or angular momentum whose principles or laws are partially expressed in what is called the Conservation of Angular Momentum. This idea was first explained in print approximately fifty years ago by Joe Dante in his groundbreaking book, *The Four Magic Moves to Winning Golf*. COAM is an integral part of Phase 7 Swing, so with Dante providing the steering wheel and the laws of physics providing the guardrails, let's take a ride down the COAM road and learn how COAM governs what we do when hitting a golf ball. And, most importantly, let's take a look at how COAM works in Phase 7 Swing.

Physics tells us that when an object rotates around a fixed axis, it rotates at a constant rate of speed provided the object stays at the same distance from the axis. If the object is brought closer to the axis, it automatically speeds up; if it is moved farther out from the axis, it slows down.

Picture a spinning figure skater that moves his arms farther away from his body, slowing his speed or, closer to his body, increasing his speed. Whichever way he positions his arms, the momentum itself is conserved. For example, with the skater's arms pinned to his chest, the momentum is distributed into the mass of his body. A corollary to this physical law is that the momentum will be distributed to the part of the system that has the lesser mass, or to the part easiest to move. This is an important principle when applied to Phase 7 Swing, and when applied to any properly executed swing.

### So how does COAM apply?

Assume that the club and player make up the mechanical system and that the axis of rotation—clockwise in Phases 1 and 2, and counterclockwise in Phases 3, 4 and 5—is the angled line created by the tilted spine. In Phases 1 and 2, when the club is raised and the body pivots clockwise, the hands, arms and club are positioned very close to the axis. When the rotational action is started in Phase 3 and continued in Phases 4 and 5, the arms and hands start down and away from the axis. As they move away from the axis, they move very quickly on the way down (aided by gravity) and continue to accelerate as they pass by the front of the rear (right) leg. All of this movement occurs in Phase 3 and the early transition to Phase 4. As the arms and hands approach impact, however, they begin to slow down. (Thanks to high speed, stop-action photography, we can confirm this phenomenon).

However, the momentum is conserved and not lost. Rather than dissipating, it feeds directly into the shaft and clubhead, thus increasing the speed of the club as it enters the impact zone. In effect, the clubhead, now the recipient of the momentum, accelerates and catches up to the hands at impact, Phase 4, and passes them in Phase 5. The momentum of the hands—a player with strong arms and hands can generate more—contributes to the speed of the club but not nearly as much speed as the law of COAM provides the clubhead. The result is speed and power at impact.

What happened? Our Phase 7 Swing harnessed one of the laws governing physical matter: The momentum was distributed to the part of the system with the lesser mass—the clubhead.

Imagine a man cracking a bullwhip, whose tip when snapped can break the speed of sound. The momentum passes from the arm, hand and butt of the whip into the steadily tapering lash to the very light tip, which has the least mass. The same principle of COAM that snaps the bullwhip, resulting in a loud crack, also governs the golf swing.

By way of a marvel of nature, a stationary round ball no more than 1.68 inches in diameter and just slightly less than 46 grams in weight can rise and soar through the air the full length of a polo field—300 yards—and beyond when it collides with a speeding, 200-gram mass of titanium fixed at the bottom of a steel shaft

Phase 6, and less that you are pushing the club with the right arm. The arms are reacting to the full pivoting of the hips and torso.

### Slow Arms, Fast Body

The biggest mass applied in the golf swing is the body, not the clubhead. The clubhead moves the fastest (see COAM on previous page) but a proper execution of Phase 7 Swing also needs the rapid rotation of the torso and hips. It does not need the rapid motion of the arms, what I call "The Flail," which often leads to swiping across the ball instead of deflecting it along the target line upon the release of the energy stored in the wrist cock (Phase 2). The clubhead receives the power; it does not create it.

Slow movement of the hips during the pivot or a rotation of the hips that is not fully completed will produce bad shots. The ball will go left—pull hooks that are the result of the arms and hands continuing through impact and beyond (Phases 4, 5 and 6), while the body or engine of the swing prematurely shuts down.

Slow-moving hips breed fast-moving hands. Fast hands can be a great asset to a magician, but they can be a double-edged sword for a golfer. Unfortunately, they often lead to a shot that is "long and wrong" because the fast-moving hands too often arrive too soon in the impact zone.

A good player, regardless of the swing system he employs, will match the speed of his hips with the speed of his hands. A strong set of hands and arms will aid in getting the club to travel faster, thus providing more power at impact. Even players with the weakest of hands, though, can generate speed with COAM.

In Phase 6, an OUT position, use the pivot to position the hands and club along the plane angle. Don't turn the

> A good player, regardless of the swing system he employs, will match the speed of his hips with the speed of his hands.

## From the Research Lab—Phase 7 Swing Affirmed

Researchers continue to study the swing with sensors, Iron Byron, computers and video. We would be remiss if we didn't consider what the camera captures, the computers compute and what those who observe record. Here are a few nuggets about the secondary role of the arms, the importance of body rotation (the pivot), and a few other swing phenomena that reflect favorably on the Phase 7 Swing principles.

1. *Backswing*—The arms do not start the backswing. The kinesic purpose of the backswing is to stretch the muscles that will propel the club.

2. *Forward swing*—The arms are taken along by the body, that is, the unwinding of the hips and upper body (the forward pivot). Without trunk rotation, a loss of motion happens that enables the body segments to transmit maximum velocity to the clubhead at impact (loss of COAM). The body can generate as much as four horsepower (using the big muscles of the trunk and legs).

3. *Pivot*—Your hip muscles are largest in the body and you must learn to use their potential power—hence, Phase 7 Swing's emphasis on the centripetal and centrifugal force of the rotary swing. When the entire body is rotating, swinging the club takes less muscular effort.

4. *Maximum COAM*—When you move the clubhead as far away from the ball as possible, as many as twenty-four feet for a John Daly-like swing arc, you create the greatest potential for maximum acceleration of the clubhead through impact. Traveling at 100 mph, a driverhead sends the ball away at about 135 mph. However, the hands are actually slowing down at impact, so a backswing that exceeds an optimum number of feet can—and will—result in less speed, diminished power and fewer yards off the tee.

pivot off till the shot is away and your eyes have looked up to locate its direction. Properly executed, the strike of your clubface will have put the ball right where you were intending it to fly.

In the downswing and through swing, Phases 3 and 4 of Phase 7 Swing, the hands lead the clubhead—they're passing the right hip while the clubhead is still 45 degrees away and they lead at impact (the shaft leans toward the target)—but the accelerating clubhead always passes the hands in Phase 5. **The accelerating clubhead is produced unconsciously by COAM but the rapid rotation of the hips and torso—begun in Phase 3, continued in Phases 4 and 5, and concluded in Phase 6—must be a conscious effort.** Remember: Phase 7 Swing cannot work with slow-turning hips or a rotation that stops in mid-turn.

### Phase 7—
### *When It Matters Not at All,*
### *the Dreaded Sideward Movement*

Thus far I have been emphasizing upward, downward and rotational movement—never sideward or lateral movement. In Phase 7, an IN position (the hands are farther from the target line along the plane angle of the swing), a slight lateral or sideward movement occurs as the swing moves to a stop. This lateral movement comes so far downstream in the sequence of phases of Phase 7 Swing that it does not diminish the quality of the swing or the power of the ballstriking. I like to remind my students, "There is no swiping, just striping . . . every time!"

Take a look at *Photos 7-4, 7-5 and 7-6.* Here is what we're looking to achieve in Phase 7: Dynamic balance controlling an upright finish with the bellybutton facing toward the target. The head moves to a level position, bringing the eyes parallel to the ground. The spine angle is re-

**7-4, 7-5** and **7-6**. Phase 7—an IN position along the plane angle of the swing.

leased from its incline and returns to perpendicular. The left leg straightens and the right knee bends. The weight of the right foot has shifted from the heel to the toe. The weight of the left foot has moved to the heel.

Congratulations! You have completed the Phase 7 Swing.

# SECTION III

# Scoring Game: Putting, Chipping and Greenside Bunker Play

*If you keep in mind that hitting firmly into the sand a couple of inches behind the ball will create a sufficient pressure to "explode" the ball out of the bunker, half your mental block will be cured. You will cure the other half simply by remembering to hit through the sand without closing the clubface. In other words, follow-through without rolling your wrists.*

*—Jack Nicklaus*

When the legendary baseball icon Branch Rickey uttered his words, "It's addition by subtraction," he could have been referring to the way Phase 7 Swing produces the various shots of golf. Learning to execute shots using Phase 7 Swing methodology is largely a matter of recognizing which phases are necessary for the particular shot (or stroke, if putting), subtracting the extraneous or unnecessary phases and then performing those that remain. For example, in executing a putt, a player doesn't need to take the club up, back or follow-through, so he would eliminate Phases 2, 3, 6 and 7.

**8-1** thru **8-4**. The putting stroke eliminates Phases 2, 3, 6 and 7. KISS—Keep It Simple Stupid.

### Putting

The putt is performed as follows:

1. Phase 1, or IN, Phase 4 (impact), or IN, and Phase 5, or IN

2. Maintain the IN position of Phase 4, when taking the putterhead back and through impact

3. Continue through to Phase 5, an IN position and conclusion of the putting stroke.

## Special Approach When Chipping on Links Courses— the Bump-and-Run

Links-style courses often demand mastery of the special variety of chipping called the bump-and-run. When your approach misses the green and rolls down into a collection area, which is common on links-style courses, you need to bump it back up the hill and run it close to the pin. Use this shot when there is no flat spot—either on the green or just short of the green—on which to land your ball, and when you can get a clean strike of the ball, that is, when it is not deep in the grass.

The exact spot of your first bounce is critical. You need to focus on this spot—usually one-half to three-quarters of the way up the hill—and land the ball where you are aiming. When this spot is properly judged and struck, the resulting bounce will take the speed off the shot, pop it up and forward, and feed the ball along the ground toward the target.

Always select an iron that you are absolutely certain will not miss hitting into the side of the hill. This strategy may mean using a five- or six-iron versus a seven-iron or using a seven-iron instead of an eight- or nine-iron. Play the ball back in your stance and stand closer, keeping 80 percent of your weight on the forward leg. Make a short swing with no weight shift, bringing the club straight back (no Phase 2 or Phase 3) and taking the club to and through impact (Phase 4 and Phase 5) with a slightly descending arc. Keep the right hand quiet, that is, do not roll the right wrist forward; this setup will preserve distance control and keep the toe from rolling over. Keep the blade square throughout the shot. Do not take a follow-through or finish the shot with the clubface moving down the target line. Avoid taking the club around to the left or up when finishing the shot.

To summarize, the Phase 7 Swing putting stroke is performed as IN-IN-IN. *See Photos 8-1, 8-2, 8-3 and 8-4.*

### Chipping
When chipping, address the ball in the middle of your

## Improving Your Overall Approach to Chipping

Here are a couple of ways you can improve your chipping:

### 1. Relocate your chipping circle

I have been told many times in my golfing career to chip to a three-foot circle around the hole. This advice has been ringing in my ears for years and I have also had many tricky downhill three-footers as a result. I have often chipped to the wrong side of the circle, with a heavy-handed shot. I don't know about you, but I would rather have an uphill six-footer than a curling, downhill, left-to-right three-footer.

Let's face it, you don't chip many balls into the hole during a round, but you do, on many occasions, fail to get up and down for your par or bogey. So let's make things easier by moving the three-foot circle to below the hole with the idea of leaving you an easier putt. You never know, you might hit the ball a little offline and actually hole out anyway.

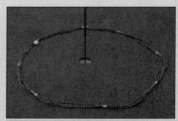

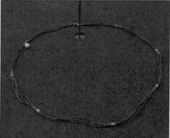

**8-5** and **8-6**. Move your imaginary three-foot circle to below the hole when chipping to a pin on a hilly green. You will finish the up-and-down with an easier uphill putt.

### 2. Cash in your chips with all your clubs

Many golfers don't realize that when it comes to selecting the best club for the special conditions of the chip, you can use virtually any club in your bag. Too many golfers are stuck on choosing a lob wedge when other clubs will do a better job.

To get the most accurate chip shot, you will want to get the ball rolling on the green as soon as possible. The more time it spends in the air, the longer it has to fly too long or too high. A chip with a lob wedge simply has less margin of error.

The rule of thumb when selecting your club is to remember that for every foot the ball is in the air, it will roll about one foot plus another in descending order. So, if you use your lob wedge, the ball will roll one foot for every foot it is in the air. If you use your nine-iron, it will roll two feet for every foot in the air. The seven-iron will roll four feet for every foot in the air, and so on.

This is a great way to estimate which club to use and to control the distance of the ball. Try it and enjoy the remarkable results.

**8-7** thru **8-10**. In chipping, subtract Phase 2 and Phase 3—the club is not raised up or behind the body, and Phases 6 and 7 (an abbreviated follow-through).

stance or setup. Here are the phases needed to executive this shot:

1. Phase 1, or IN, Phase 4 (impact), or IN, and Phase 5, or IN

2. In Phase 5, the face does not close or roll forward and over. Loft is retained on the clubface. *See Photos 8-7, 8-8, 8-9 and 8-10.*

To envision the execution of a chip shot, remember to use addition by subtraction. Subtract Phase 2 and Phase 3 (the club is not raised up to the shoulder level or behind the body), as well as Phases 6 and 7 (there is an abbreviated follow-through toward the target and not around the front of the body).

### Greenside Bunker Play

Traditional bunker shot technique calls for an open stance, an open clubface aimed at the target and a swing along the line formed by the feet. Phase 7 Swing technique is much simpler. Take a normal address position, feet aligned parallel to the target line instead of to the left of it, and the leading edge of the club square or perpendicular to the target line. To play the shot, execute the swing as follows:

1. Perform Phase 1, an IN position

2. Violate Phase 2, that is, do not exchange positions of the hands and clubface along the swing plane and allow the clubhead to move toward vertical in the takeaway

3. Violate Phase 3, that is, release the clubhead early in the forward swing in lieu of building lag as required in non-greenside bunker shots

4. Execute Phase 4, an IN position at impact

5. Violate Phase 5, that is, let the clubhead move past the hands in a scooping action through the sand after impact

6. Execute Phase 6, an OUT position, keeping the body

## Adjust for Sand Conditions

Good results from a sand bunker, like good results on the putting green, depend greatly on your ability to "read the sand," much as you would "read the green." Use your feet and eyes. Walk to the ball and assume your stance will give you opportunities to learn about the sand's depth, its degree of firmness (fluffy or packed) and whether it is coarse or granular, dry or wet.

Sand conditions, once studied and determined, call for adjustments. If the sand is hard or wet, you need to guard against having the clubhead bounce off the sand and into the ball. With a sand wedge or lob wedge, square up the clubface, which diminishes the bounce of the sole, and make sure you enter the sand with the front edge of the club leading.

If the sand is coarse or wet it will also be firmer, which will cause more bounce upon the club's entry. A club bouncing off a firm surface will skid forward and strike the ball with leading edge, causing a skulled shot, which you don't want to do! For a ball resting on wet sand, use the leading edge of your club to dig. Failing to use the leading edge of the club is one of the most common mistakes made when hitting from a wet sand bunker.

If the sand is fluffy or dry, your club will dig and slide more easily under the ball. For a ball on soft sand, use more of the back edge (bounce) of your club. If the sand is dry and fluffy, avoid digging too far into the sand by opening the clubface and using the back edge. Adjust by gripping down an inch on the grip and stabilize your feet by digging into the sand an inch or two.

Varying the depth of the cut and speed of the swing can control distance. If you make a deeper cut, the ball will fly shorter and higher. If you made a shallower cut, the ball will fly longer and lower. Vary the depth of the cut by cocking the club up in the backswing. For a shallower cut, use less cocking in the backswing. A slower swing will cut down distance just as a faster swing will add carry. An easy way to regulate the speed or force of your swing is to focus on carrying the length of your follow-through. A shorter follow-through will cut down on the shot's distance, while a longer one will carry the ball farther.

**8-11** thru **8-14**. Remember that Phase 7 Swing's bunker technique requires a different address and setup to the ball. Take a normal address position, feet aligned parallel to the target line and the leading edge square to the target line.

turning through the shot and allowing the right hip to come around past the point of impact

7. Eliminate Phase 7, an IN position.

*See Photos 8-11, 8-12, 8-13 and 8-14.*

# 9

## Working the Ball: Hitting the Fade and the Draw

*It's no accident that some of the best drivers in the game have used the fade as their bread-and-butter shot. Sam Snead, Ben Hogan, Jack Nicklaus and Lee Trevino, just to name a few, are among the most accurate drivers in history, and all are notorious for fading the ball when they had to hit the fairway.*

*—Corey Pavin*

A fade is a shot where the ball flies intentionally from left to right. It is used in many kinds of situations: 1. The prevailing wind is blowing right to left and you want to "hold" the shot against this breeze; 2. The shot is impeded by an obstacle, often a tree, and you must curve the ball around the tree from left to right; 3. The green is severely sloped from right to left with a pin placement in the right hemisphere of the green, which demands a shot that will move to the right after landing; 4. The green surface is hard and fast, and will receive best results with a shot with a high trajectory and softer landing (as opposed to a draw, which tends to land "hotter" and roll more after landing).

**9-1** and **9-2**. When hitting a fade move the ball about an inch forward and an inch inward.

### Phase 7 Swing Fade Techniques

Hitting a fade calls for no changes, no addition by subtraction, of the phases. Simply move the ball forward and in, about an inch forward and an inch inward. The ball should be opposite the heel of the club at address. Take your normal address and your normal swing. You will strike the ball farther along the arc with the club moving slightly left, away from the centerline of the arc, as it strikes the ball. This offline deflection or contact will produce a shot that curves from left to right—a fade. *See Photos 9-1 and 9-2.*

### Hitting the Draw

The legendary Bobby Jones had a special affection for the draw. According to Jones, "The draw almost always adds a good many yards to the drive, and it is, for me at any rate, far more satisfactory in playing a long boring iron shot to the green. Further, a familiarity with its use does more than anything else to overcome one of the most troublesome things in golf—a hard crosswind off the left side of the fairway."

Remember, a draw moves from right to left with a

**9-3** and **9-4**. When hitting a draw move the ball back approximately two inches and in approximately one inch. Set the toe of the club opposite the ball. Contact the inside part of the ball.

gentle curl. A hook veers immediately and severely from right to left from the point of contact. Generally, the draw,

## Maintain Your Spine Angle

One common mistake that golfers make when swinging is a failure to maintain their spine angle. If golfers did not tilt forward from the hips, that is, if they swung without bending, it's unlikely that this mistake would occur. Picture a baseball player hitting a pitch at shoulder height—the batter's pivot would require the shoulders to stay parallel to the ground while turning around the axis of the spine, which remained at 90 degrees, or perpendicular to the ground.

That mistake is not possible, however, with a Phase 7 Swing, or any golf swing. The golfer must bend at the hips, approximately 30 degrees from perpendicular, to hit the ball that is on the ground. Good players maintain this spine angle throughout the backswing by turning their shoulders level to their spine. While tilted forward to a position of approximately 60 degrees (30 degrees from perpendicular), the shoulders and core of the body rotate around the spine. At the top, the left shoulder is lower than the right because the spine angle is tilted toward the ground.

which is better behaved than a hook, is the shot you want in your bag.

In hitting a draw with Phase 7 Swing technique, simply move the ball back approximately two inches and in, under the imaginary target line, one inch. *See Photos 9-3 and 9-4.* The ball at address should be opposite the toe of your club. When executing the shot, swing along the line created by your stance but concentrate at impact on contacting the inside part of the ball, thus creating a ballstrike that creates a right-to-left trajectory.

# Glossary

**Acceleration**
A measure of how fast velocity increases with time

**Angular Momentum**
A measure of the tendency of an object to keep rotating, or moving, in a circle

**Angular Motion**
The movement of an object around an axis, the speed of which it is rotating is called angular velocity

**Axis**
An imaginary straight line about which an object rotates, such as the shoulders rotating round the spine. More broadly, a center of principal structure about which something turns or is arranged.

**Axis Tilt**
A change—a bending backward away from the target—of the axis of the spine during the downswing. This motion is not produced in a Phase 7 Swing.

**Back is Up**
In taking the club back from address, one moves the club straight up by extending the bottom of the left wrist down on the handle (extending it toward the target line), thus moving

the clubshaft from incline to horizontal to incline to vertical to incline, a position traditionally referred to as "at the top of the backswing"

### Behind the Ball
This is the position attained by the clubhead at the termination of Phase 1 and beginning of Phase 2, traditionally referred to as "the top of the backswing"

### Center of Gravity
The point at which gravity can be considered to act

### Centrifugal Force
The outward force on a body moving in a curved or circular path around another body

### Centripetal Force
The inward or "center-seeking" force on a body moving in a circle or curved path around another body

### Coefficient of Restitution
A fractional value representing the ratio of speeds after and before an impact of two colliding bodies. For two objects to register a COR of zero, the objects would "stop" at the collision, not bouncing at all.

### Conservation of Angular Momentum
The holding on to the momentum of an object rotating around an axis

### Deceleration
A measure of how fast velocity decreases with time

### Dynamic
Objects in motion

### Dynamic Balance
The state of equilibrium in the golfer's pivot around to the back and around to the front

### Energy
An exertion of power or intense action

## Force
A push or pull on an object that tends to make it move. The force can be a body or contact force.

## Friction
A force between an object and the ground, which always acts to opposite of the object. In golf, the force opposing the pressure of the feet on the ground when pivoting.

## Gravity
The force of attraction between two bodies. Earth's gravity is the force of attraction of a mass close to its surface toward its center.

## Ground Reaction Force
The force that the ground applies back to the golfer, an application of Newton's Third Law (force occurs in pairs, equal in size but opposite in direction)

## In
The positioning of the hands along the swing plane farther away from the target line than the clubhead. Phase 7 Swing has four IN positions: 1, 4, 5 and 7.

## Inclined Plane
A flat surface of any extent positioned between horizontal and vertical

## Inertia
Resistance of an object to change in velocity. It is the tendency of an object to remain at rest, or to continue to move in the same direction at constant speed unless it is acted upon by an external force, such as friction. The greater the inertia, the more resistant the object is to either an increase or decrease in velocity.

## Kinetic Energy
The energy possessed by a system or body as a result of its motion

## Lateral Shift
The movement of the entire body, either backward or forward, along a line parallel to the target line, which is often a cause of

faulty strikes of the ball and always a source of power leakage. You will not produce this movement in Phase 7 Swing.

### Loft
Backward slope, measured in degrees, of the face of a golf club's head

### Mass
A measure of the amount of matter in an object. The mass of an object is also a measure of the amount of inertia that mass possesses, such as its resistance to change when moving.

### Moment of Inertia
A measure of an object's resistance to rotation; it is analogous to inertia, an object's resistance to change in linear velocity. The rotational inertia depends on the mass of the object, the shape of the object and how the mass is distributed throughout the object's shape. The farther away the mass of an object is from the axis of rotation—in the case of a golf swing, your hands—the harder it is to swing the object.

### Newton's First Law
An object in motion will remain in motion until it is acted upon by an outside force. In the absence of an external force, an object will maintain its velocity or state of rest.

### Newton's Second Law
The acceleration an object equals the mass of an object multiplied by its net force. As the force acting upon an object is increased, the acceleration of the object is increased. As the mass of an object is increased, the acceleration of the object is decreased. Thus, the acceleration of an object depends directly upon the net force acting upon the object, and inversely upon the mass of the object.

### Newton's Third Law
For every action force there is an equal (in size) and opposite (in direction) reaction force

### Out
The positioning of the hands closer along the swing plane to the target line than the clubhead. Phase 7 Swing has three OUT positions: 2, 3 and 6.

**Physics**
The science of matter and energy and their interactions

**Pivot**
The motion of a body moving around a center point

**Plane**
A flat surface, either real or imagined

**Plane Angle**
The imaginary line formed between 1. the ball at rest at address and 2. the clubhead and shaft at the top of the backswing. In Phase 7 Swing, it does not rise above the shoulders.

**Plane Line**
The imaginary line at the base of the plane angle; when extended from the ball toward the target, it forms the target line.

**Radial Flexion**
Referring to the left wrist appearing flat or bowed

**Rotary Swing**
A swing characterized by tightly turning the entire body—the legs, core and upper body—around a fixed axis without swaying the body off center, that is, without moving the head and spine laterally along a line parallel to the target line

**Transverse**
Crosswise or at-right angles. The transverse angle in one's body is formed by a 90-degree intersection of the spinal column.

**Velocity**
Speed and direction of motion of a moving body.

**Violate**
When hitting a special shot, such as a greenside bunker shot, the omission of a phase of Phase 7 Swing

**Width**
The maximum distance or arc of the clubhead attained at the top of the backswing. It builds steadily during Phase 1 and terminates as Phase 2 commences.

# Index

and greenside bunker play, 122, 124
leaning toward, 41
left knee moving toward, 64, 72, 86,
    89
low and slow takeaway long, 82
pushing club straight back along,
    60–61
and swing practice station, 59
target practice, 56, 101
targets, hitting shots to, 101
tee shots, 98
tempo and warm-up, 84
thin shots, 82–83
tomahawk effect, 61
trajectory and carry vs. roll
    components of shots, 59
transverse body pivot, 7–8
transverse plane of the body, 70
trapping the ball, 97

**U**
upswing/backswing pivot

hands below shoulder, 86–88
and kinetic chain, 71
left wrist takes the club up, 31–32
"low and slow" vs., 29, 57–59, 60,
    62–63
pivot stays over the ball, 40–41
pivot takes the club back, 31, 32, 34
terminology of, 91–93
*See also* Phase 1; Phase 2; Phase 3

**W**
warm-up practice, 56, 84
Weedon, Reeves, 7–8
weight distribution, 85–88, 106–7
weight shifts, 40–41, 69–70
width (getting behind the ball), 54–60,
    82
wrists, cocking the, 46, 83–85. *See also*
    left wrist

# *For beginners, Phase 7 Swing is a map.*

## Want to Hit it Like the Pros?

## Play Consistent Golf?

## Improve Your Game?

Join us at a golf venue near you. Reeves Weedon and his groundbreaking Phase 7 Swing laws and techniques are sponsoring small-group, one-day clinics in several key locations.

• When you sign up for a Phase 7 Swing Golf Clinic—which will be held at a golf sites serving students in Florida, New England, Mid-Atlantic States, and the Carolinas—you will learn golf's most rotational golf swing, the most efficient and powerful way to swing a golf club and the game's simplest way to better overall golf.

• You will learn how to use the ground to add power and distance, how to properly put loft on the club, and how to set the club on the true plane of the right forearm and deliver the club through impact along that plane.

• Plus, a special take-home practice routine that will enable you to learn Phase 7 Swing with guaranteed certainty and instant feedback.

Contact information:

Internet:     www.phase7swing.com

Phone:      011 44 208 421 7266  (From U.S. to U.K.)

*...for advanced players, a compass!*

## Become a Certified Instructor
## of the Phase 7 Swing

Reeves Weedon is conducting clinics for fellow professionals who want to enhance their teaching with the techniques of Phase 7 Swing.

- Learn how to get your students hitting more consistent shots

- Understand how to harness Newton's laws of motion for more distance off the tee

- Show your students how to employ the power of the left wrist

- Discover the true meaning of "getting behind the ball" and watch how this    improves your students' ballstriking

Phase 7 Swing clinics for teaching professionals will be coming to a site near you—in Florida, New England, Mid-Atlantic States and the Carolinas.  Inquire about registration, schedule and fees by contacting Reeves Weedon at the following:

Internet:    www.phase7swing

Phone:    011 44 208 421 7266  (From U.S. to U.K.)

"I'm in the business of going long . . . but not wrong. When I needed an edge, the confidence that I was converting every bit of my energy into power, I went to Reeves Weedon, who showed me how. I am striping it longer and straighter than ever, and I know why."

—Joe Miller, *2010 RE/MAX World Long Drive Champion*

For the novice golfer, Phase 7 Swing is a map; for the experienced player, it is a compass.

—Ian Clark, *Fellow of the P.G.A.*

"When you meet Reeves Weedon, you realize that not many other golf instructors have such an indisputable passion and a tireless work ethic. Reeves's Phase 7 Swing has many unique elements, including an exclusive way of utilizing the body throughout the stroke. It also replicates the swing traits we've seen in some of golf's all-time great ballstrikers. Reeves taught me to understand the things (in the swing) that we don't see."

—James Dowling, *PGA*